From our Kitchen to Yours

Suppers in a Snap

Quick-to-fix dinners, sides & desserts plus lots of time-saving tips

*To cooks everywhere
who know that a steamy hot
casserole or a warm bubbly
dessert can warm the heart
as well as fill the tummy.*

Gooseberry Patch
An imprint of Globe Pequot
246 Goose Lane
Guilford, CT 06437

www.gooseberrypatch.com
1 800 854 6673

•••••••••••••••••••••

Do you have a tried & true recipe...
tip, craft or memory that you'd like to
see featured in a **Gooseberry Patch**
cookbook? Visit our website at www.
gooseberrypatch.com and follow the
easy steps to submit your favorite
family recipe.

Or send them to us at:
Gooseberry Patch
PO Box 812
Columbus, OH 43216-0812

Don't forget to include the number
of servings your recipe makes, plus
your name, address, phone number
and email address. If we select your
recipe, your name will appear right
along with it... and you'll receive a
FREE copy of the book!

CONTENTS

Our favorite tips for quick & easy cooking

Sometimes getting dinner on the table when you're short on time takes more than a good recipe. It takes knowing just a few helpful tips to get ingredients prepped and ready to go. Whether you're cooking up a quick-to-fix slow-cooker meal, a 5-ingredient recipe, or a quick-to-cook supper, handy tips can help you save precious minutes. Here are some of our favorite time-saving tips for getting a tasty meal ready in a jiffy:

Read your recipe top to bottom before starting to cook. You might be tempted to skip this important step when you're in a rush, but don't! Making sure you have all of the ingredients and knowing cooking times in advance is an essential first step..

Gather all of your ingredients before you begin. Small bowls or muffin tins are handy kitchen helpers. It's another helpful way to make sure you've got everything you need before you start.

Eat the skin! Not all produce needs to be peeled before cooking. Wash your produce well, but if it has thin skin, don't bother peeling. Potatoes, beets, carrots and sweet potatoes are just a few of the veggies that taste great with the skin on.

Use parchment paper. Roast all your veggies on parchment paper and clean-up is a snap!

Cook extra and freeze it. Roast two chickens, brown double batches of ground beef, make double batches of soup and rice. Weeknight meals are fast and easy when you've already got some extra ingredients in the freezer.

Clean as you go. Rinse prep bowls and utensils as you go. Fill the sink with warm, soapy water and they'll be easier to clean before you load the dishwasher.

Reuben Appetizers, Page 28

CHAPTER ONE

Appetizers & Beverages

Greek Olive Cups, Page 16

Fruit & Nut Cheese Log, Page 24

Roseanne Cranston, St. Louis, MO

Texas Caviar

This dip is a hands-down crowd-pleaser. Serve it with your favorite multi-colored tortilla chips.

Makes 4 cups.

15-oz. can black beans, drained
    and rinsed
15-oz. can black-eyed peas, drained
    and rinsed
15-1/4 oz. can corn, drained
16-oz. jar salsa
Optional: chopped fresh cilantro

Stir together all ingredients except cilantro; transfer to an airtight container. Refrigerate several hours before serving. Garnish with cilantro, if desired.

Leona Krivda, Belle Vernon, PA

Marcie's Autumn Tea

My oldest daughter makes this refreshing chilled tea in the fall and it is always a hit.

Makes about 3 quarts.

5 tea bags
1/2 c. sugar
5 c. boiling water
5 c. unsweetened apple juice
2 c. cranberry juice cocktail
1/3 c. lemon juice
1/4 t. pumpkin pie spice
ice cubes

Combine tea bags and sugar in a heat-proof one-gallon pitcher. Add boiling water; let stand for 8 minutes. Discard tea bags. Add juices and spice; stir well until sugar is dissolved. Chill; serve over ice.

★ TIME-SAVING SHORTCUT ★ Make some lemony iced tea and let it chill overnight. It'll be ready in a jiffy for lunch or dinner the next day! Brew 9 tea bags in 3 quarts boiling water for 5 minutes. Discard tea bags. Stir in a 12-ounce can of frozen lemonade concentrate and a cup of sugar. Serve over ice...ahh!

Texas Caviar

Robyn Wright, Delaware, OH

Bacon-Wrapped Scallops

Wrapped in bacon strips, these succulent scallops will be snapped up quickly! Be sure to buy sea scallops, which are larger in diameter than the smaller bay scallops.

Makes 22 appetizers.

11 slices bacon, cut in half
1/2 c. all-purpose flour
1-1/2 t. paprika
1/2 t. salt
1/2 t white pepper
1/2 t. garlic powder
1 c. milk
1 egg
22 sea scallops
1 to 2 c. panko bread crumbs
Optional: cocktail sauce

In a skillet over medium heat, cook bacon slices for 3 to 4 minutes, until translucent; drain. Combine flour and seasonings in a shallow dish. Beat together milk and egg in a small bowl. Roll scallops in seasoned flour, shaking off excess. Dip scallops in egg mixture, then coat with bread crumbs. Wrap each scallop with bacon and secure with a toothpick.

Place scallops on a lightly greased baking sheet. Bake at 400 degrees for about 30 minutes, until bacon is crisp and scallops are cooked through. Serve hot with cocktail sauce, if desired.

Rosalyn Smith, Apache Junction, AZ

Zesty Chili Dip

My husband shared this dip recipe with me at our first camping experience as a new family. It's speedy to make and hearty enough to be a meal. I'm sure you will like it too!

Serves 5 to 10.

1 lb. ground beef
16-oz. pkg. Mexican pasteurized process cheese spread, cubed
15-oz. can hot chili with beans
15-oz. can chili with no beans
tortilla chips

Brown beef in a skillet over medium heat; drain. Add cheese and chili to skillet; reduce heat. Simmer for about 10 minutes, stirring occasionally, until cheese is melted. Serve warm with tortilla chips.

Bacon-Wrapped Scallops

Jackie Barr, Ontario, OH

Tomato Cocktail

Serve this great appetizer drink for your guests to enjoy while you're putting the finishing touches on dinner.

Serves 6.

46-oz. can tomato juice
juice of 1/2 lemon
1 t. sweet onion, grated
1 t. Worcestershire sauce
1/8 t. hot pepper sauce
Garnish: celery sticks

Combine all ingredients except celery sticks in a large pitcher; stir well and chill. Garnish each serving with a celery stick.

Ashley Connelly, Louisa, VA

Fruit Salsa with Cinnamon Chips

I made this for our Sunday morning church refreshments and it was a huge hit! I also like to take this to bridal and baby showers.

Serves 10 to 15.

2 kiwi, peeled and diced
2 Golden Delicious apples, peeled, cored and diced
1/2 lb. raspberries
1 lb. strawberries, hulled and diced
1 c. plus 2 T. sugar, divided
1 T. brown sugar, packed
3 T. strawberry preserves
1 to 2 T. cinnamon
10 10-inch flour tortillas, sliced into wedges

Combine all fruit in a large bowl; mix in 2 tablespoons sugar, brown sugar and strawberry preserves. Cover and chill at least 15 minutes. In a separate bowl, mix together remaining sugar and cinnamon. Arrange tortilla wedges in a single layer on an ungreased baking sheet; coat chips with butter-flavored vegetable spray. Sprinkle with desired amount of cinnamon-sugar. Bake at 350 degrees for 8 to 10 minutes. Repeat with remaining tortilla wedges; cool 15 minutes. Serve chips with chilled fruit mixture.

Fruit Salsa with Cinnamon Chips

Stephanie Norton, Saginaw, TX

Nana's Slow-Cooker Meatballs

Makes 4 dozen.

2-1/2 c. catsup
1 c. brown sugar, packed
2 T. Worcestershire sauce
2 lbs. ground beef
1.35-oz. pkg. onion soup mix
5-oz. can evaporated milk

Combine catsup, brown sugar and Worcestershire sauce in a 4-quart slow cooker; stir well and cover. Turn slow cooker to high setting and allow mixture to warm while preparing the meatballs. Combine beef, onion soup mix and evaporated milk; mix well and form into one-inch balls. Place meatballs on an ungreased 15"x10" jelly-roll pan. Bake at 325 degrees for 20 minutes; drain. Spoon meatballs into slow cooker and reduce setting to low. Cover and cook 2 to 3 hours, stirring gently after one hour.

Lisa Herold, Abilene, TX

Ham & Olive Roll-Ups

This is a yummy snack for anyone on the go! A neighbor gave me this recipe during the holidays.

Serves 4 to 6.

1 lb. deli sliced ham
2 8-oz. pkgs. cream cheese, softened
Optional: 1 T. pimentos, minced
4-1/2 oz. can whole black olives, drained

Pat ham slices dry with a paper towel. Spread cream cheese over one side of each ham slice. Sprinkle with pimentos, if desired. Roll up ham slice jelly-roll style; slice into one-inch thick pieces. Fasten each roll with a toothpick topped with an olive. Serve immediately or refrigerate until serving time.

★ TIME-SAVING SHORTCUT ★ Replace ground beef, soup mix and milk in Nana's Slow-Cooker Meatballs with a 26-ounce package of frozen meatballs. Add meatballs to sauce in slow cooker and cook on high 2 to 3 hours.

Nana's Slow-Cooker Meatballs

JoAnn, Gooseberry Patch

Monterey Mushroom Squares

These cheesy squares are irresistible! Mix & match different kinds of mushrooms and cheeses for variety.

Makes 2 dozen.

8-oz. tube refrigerated crescent rolls
2 c. sliced mushrooms
1/4 c. butter, melted
1/2 c. shredded Monterey Jack cheese
1/2 t. dried oregano
1/4 t. onion salt

Separate rolls into 2 long rectangles. Press into the bottom and 1/2-inch up the sides of a lightly greased 13"x9" baking pan. Toss mushrooms with melted butter; spoon over dough. Sprinkle with remaining ingredients. Bake, uncovered, at 375 degrees for 20 to 25 minutes. Cut into squares; serve warm.

Beth Bainbridge, Tulsa, OK

Greek Olive Cups

These are different from the usual appetizers and are a breeze to make.

Makes 2-1/2 dozen.

1-1/2 c. shredded Cheddar cheese, divided
1/2 c. green olives, chopped
1/2 c. Kalamata olives, pitted and chopped
1/3 c. chopped pecans, toasted
1/3 c. pine nuts, toasted
2-1/2 T. mayonnaise
2 2.1-oz. pkgs. frozen mini phyllo shells

Combine one cup cheese and remaining ingredients except phyllo shells; mix well and set aside. Remove phyllo shells from packages, leaving them in trays. Spoon one heaping teaspoon of cheese mixture into each phyllo shell; sprinkle evenly with remaining cheese. Remove cups from trays and place on an ungreased baking sheet. Bake at 375 degrees for 12 to 15 minutes, until heated through. Serve immediately.

★ FREEZE IT ★ These tasty cups can be made ahead and frozen. Fill the cups in their trays, then place the trays in heavy-duty plastic zipping bags and freeze them up to one month. When ready to bake, remove the cups from their trays and place them on an ungreased baking sheet. Let the cups stand 10 minutes before baking. Bake as directed in the recipe.

Greek Olive Cups

Jane Moore, Haverford, PA

Crab & Broccoli Rolls

Season these rolls with onion or garlic salt to taste, or spice them up with a dash of hot pepper sauce.

Makes 8 rolls.

6-oz. can crabmeat, drained
 and flaked
10-oz. pkg. frozen chopped broccoli,
 cooked, drained and cooled
1/4 c. mayonnaise
1/2 c. shredded Swiss cheese
8-oz. tube refrigerated crescent rolls,
 separated

Combine crabmeat, broccoli, mayonnaise and cheese. Spread about 2 tablespoons on each crescent. Roll up crescent roll-style; arrange on a lightly greased baking sheet. Bake at 375 degrees for 18 to 20 minutes, until golden.

Tammy McCarthy, Oxford, OH

Broiled Cheese Rounds

These make tasty after-school snacks too.

Makes 2-1/2 dozen.

1 lb. bacon, crisply cooked and
 crumbled
1 lb. shredded sharp Cheddar cheese
1 onion, minced
1 to 2 T. mayonnaise
2 loaves sliced party rye bread

In a medium mixing bowl, combine bacon, cheese and onion; blend in mayonnaise. Spread mixture onto bread slices; place on an ungreased baking sheet. Broil 3 to 4 inches from heat source for 3 minutes.

★ SIMPLE INGREDIENT SWAP ★ **Make these cheese rounds veggie-friendly by replacing the bacon with a 16-ounce package of sliced mushrooms, sautéed until golden.**

Crab & Broccoli Rolls

Janice Dorsey, San Antonio, TX

Glazed Cocktail Sausages

Put these savory sausages in your slow cooker the morning of the big football game...they'll be ready by kickoff!

Serves 16 to 20.

2 16-oz. pkgs. mini smoked sausages
1 c. apricot preserves
1/2 c. maple syrup
2 T. bourbon or 1 to 2 t. vanilla extract

Combine all ingredients in an ungreased 3-quart slow cooker. Cover and cook on low setting for 4 hours.

Jennifer Apthorpe, Panama, NY

Holiday Stuffed Mushrooms

Start a memorable holiday tradition by making these mouthwatering mushroom tidbits.

Serves 6 to 8.

8-oz. pkg. cream cheese, softened
1 T. dried, minced onion
2 t. Worcestershire sauce
1 lb. bacon, crisply cooked and
   crumbled
1-1/2 lbs. mushrooms, stems removed

Combine cream cheese, onion and Worcestershire sauce in a bowl. Beat with an electric mixer on medium-high speed until thoroughly blended. Stir in bacon; fill mushroom caps with mixture. Arrange on an ungreased baking sheet. Bake at 375 degrees for 15 minutes, or until tops of mushrooms are golden.

★ SIMPLE INGREDIENT SWAP ★
Out of apricot preserves? Use whatever preserves you have on hand. Cherry, grape and raspberry would all work well with cocktail sausages!

Holiday Stuffed Mushrooms

Lynda Robson, Boston, MA

Fruity Spiced Tea

Enliven a gray day with this delicious and colorful blend of fruit juices and spices.

Makes 3 quarts.

6 c. boiling water
1 T. unsweetened instant tea mix
1/2 t. allspice
1/2 t. cinnamon
1/2 t. nutmeg
3-oz. pkg. cherry gelatin mix
1 c. orange juice
1/4 c. lemon juice
4 c. cranberry juice cocktail
1/2 c. sugar
Garnish: orange slices

Pour boiling water into a heat-proof pitcher. Stir in tea and spices; steep 5 minutes. Stir in gelatin mix; let cool. Add juices and sugar; stir until sugar dissolves. Chill and serve over ice; garnish with orange slices.

Kay Pyle, Stockton, MO

Country Caviar

One of our favorite dips! It's easy to make and keeps for days in the fridge, if it lasts that long. I have made it for ages and my grandkids love it. Spice it to suit to your taste, from mild to extra hot.

Serves 8 to 10.

15-oz. can black, red or pinto beans, drained
11-oz. can sweet corn & diced peppers, drained
10-oz. can mild, medium or hot diced tomatoes with green chiles, drained
6 green onions, chopped
2 c. shredded Monterey Jack, Pepper Jack or Cheddar cheese
1 c. light mayonnaise
1 c. light sour cream
hot pepper sauce to taste
pita chips, tortilla chips

Mix together all ingredients except chips in a large bowl. Cover and chill; may be kept refrigerated for several days. Serve with warm pita chips or tortilla chips.

★ SIMPLE INGREDIENT SWAP ★ Make mayo go the extra mile! Flavor it with crushed garlic, chopped fresh herbs, lemon juice or even ready-made pesto.

Fruity Spiced Tea

Becky Stewart, Alliance, OH

Slow-Cooker Sweet-and-Sour Meatballs

Great as bite-size appetizers...you can also enjoy them as meatball sandwiches.

Serves 10 to 15.

16-oz. can cranberry sauce
12-oz. jar chili sauce
2 T. brown sugar, packed
2-lb. pkg. frozen Italian meatballs

In a saucepan, combine cranberry sauce, chili sauce and brown sugar. Cook over medium heat until warmed through; stir well. Place meatballs in a 4-quart slow cooker; add sauce mixture and stir to coat meatballs. Cover and cook on high setting for about 2 hours, or on low setting for about 6 hours, until heated through.

Sharon Demers, Dolores, CO

Fruit & Nut Cheese Log

Cream cheese, fruit and nuts give this easy-to-make starter a unique zing of flavor.

Serves 8 to 10.

8-oz. pkg. cream cheese, softened
1 T. apple jelly
1/4 c. dried apricots, chopped
1/4 c. dried tart cherries, chopped
1/4 c. chopped walnuts
wheat crackers or fresh fruit

Place cream cheese on a sheet of plastic wrap; top with a second sheet of plastic wrap. Use a rolling pin to roll cheese into an 8-inch by 6-inch rectangle, about 1/2-inch thick. Remove top sheet of plastic wrap and discard. Spread jelly over cheese; sprinkle with dried fruits. Gently roll into a log, jelly-roll style. Roll log in chopped walnuts and wrap in plastic wrap; refrigerate until ready to serve. Place log on a serving plate; serve with wheat crackers and fresh fruit.

★ TIME-SAVING SHORTCUT ★
Need to soften cream cheese in a hurry? Simply place an unwrapped 8-ounce block on a plate and microwave for about a minute at 50% power.

Fruit & Nut Cheese Log

Jean Cerutti, Kittanning, PA

Can't-Miss Creamy Beef Dip

Everyone will beg you for this recipe... it's a yummy, fast alternative to the traditional cheese ball.

Serves 15 to 20.

2 8-oz. pkgs. cream cheese, softened
8-oz. container spreadable Cheddar
  cheese
8-oz. pkg. shredded Cheddar cheese
1 bunch green onions, finely chopped
5-oz. jar dried beef, finely chopped
2 T. Worcestershire sauce
assorted crackers or chips

Blend cheeses together in a bowl. Add onions, beef and sauce; mix well. Cover and refrigerate at least 2 hours. Serve with crackers or chips.

Jeannie Garton, Duxbury, MA

Orange Slushy

Refresh yourself with a glass of soothing orange goodness.

Serves 2 to 3.

6-oz. can frozen orange juice
  concentrate
1/4 c. sugar
1 c. milk
1 t. vanilla extract
12 ice cubes

Combine all ingredients in a blender; blend to desired consistency.

★ TIME-SAVING SHORTCUT ★ This Creamy Beef Dip can be made the night before. Keep covered until ready to serve.

Orange Slushy

Charlotte Smith, Tyrone, PA

Cranberry Chutney-Brie Appetizers

These little bite-sized tidbits are so tasty and yummy!

Serves 10 to 12.

12-oz. brie cheese, rind removed
2 2.1-oz. pkgs. frozen flaky layer
    biscuits
1/4 c. whole-berry cranberry sauce
1 T. glazed walnuts, chopped

Cut brie into 1/4-inch cubes. Bake biscuits according to package instructions. With a serrated knife, split biscuits. Place biscuits cut-side up on an ungreased baking sheet. Arrange cheese cubes on top of biscuits; spoon cranberry sauce over top. Sprinkle with walnuts. Bake at 375 degrees for 3 to 5 minutes, or until cheese is softened and warm. Cut each biscuit into quarters.

Carol Hickman, Kingsport, TN

Reuben Appetizers

Put these mini Reubens together in minutes, and they'll be gone in seconds!

Makes one dozen.

1 loaf sliced party rye bread
1/2 c. Thousand Island salad dressing
3/4 lb. sliced corned beef
14-oz. can sauerkraut, drained
1-1/2 c. shredded Swiss cheese

Spread bread slices on one side with salad dressing; set aside. Cut corned beef to fit bread; place 2 slices on each bread slice. Top each with one to 2 teaspoons sauerkraut; sprinkle with cheese. Arrange bread slices on an ungreased baking sheet. Bake at 350 degrees for 10 minutes, or until cheese melts.

★ SIMPLE INGREDIENT SWAP ★ These Reuben appetizers taste just as delicious with sliced pastrami, ham or even roast beef.

Reuben Appetizers

Margaret Collins, Clarendon Hills, IL

Chicken-Salsa Dip

Scoop it out with tortilla chips or corn chips...a perfect appetizer for a small gathering!

Serves 8.

8-oz. pkg. cream cheese, softened
8-oz. jar salsa, divided
8-oz. pkg. shredded Mexican-blend cheese
2 to 3 boneless, skinless chicken breasts, cooked and diced
tortilla chips

Blend cream cheese with half of the salsa; spread in the bottom of an ungreased 9" pie plate. Top with remaining salsa; sprinkle with cheese and chicken. Bake, uncovered, at 350 degrees for 25 minutes, until hot and cheese is melted. Serve warm with tortilla chips.

Beverly Weppler, Atlantic, IA

Spunky Spinach Dip

To add extra spice to this tasty dip, use medium to hot salsa.

Serves 10.

2 c. salsa
2 c. shredded Monterey Jack cheese
8-oz. pkg. cream cheese, softened and cubed
10-oz. pkg. frozen chopped spinach, thawed and drained
1 c. black olives, chopped

Mix together all ingredients in a microwave-safe bowl; stir well. Microwave on medium setting until heated through.

★ TIME-SAVING SHORTCUT ★ Try using a store-bought rotisserie chicken to save loads of time for this Chicken-Salsa Dip!

Chicken-Salsa Dip

Bonnie Waters, Bloomington, IN

Cranberry-Jalapeño Salsa

This salsa has been a family favorite at Thanksgiving and other gatherings for many years. I have to make two or three batches! We grow our own jalapeños and green onions, so when in season, it's fresh from our garden. This salsa is also delicious as a sauce over roast turkey or pork for a meal or sandwich.

Makes 8 servings.

14-oz. can whole-berry cranberry
   sauce
1 jalapeño pepper, halved, seeded and
   diced
1/4 c. fresh cilantro, snipped
2 green onions, sliced
1 t. lime juice
1/4 t. ground cumin
tortilla chips

In a bowl, combine all ingredients except tortilla chips. Stir until well blended. Serve at room temperature or cover and chill. Serve with tortilla chips.

Jessica Parker, Mulvane, KS

Sweetheart Shakes

Surprise your sweetheart with a frosty and refreshing two-tone shake!

Serves 4.

3 c. milk, divided
1 c. vanilla ice cream, softened
3-1/2 oz. pkg. instant vanilla pudding
   mix, divided
1 c. strawberry ice cream, softened
3 drops red food coloring

Pour 1-1/2 cups milk into a blender; add vanilla ice cream and 1/3 of dry pudding mix. Cover; blend on high until smooth, about 15 seconds. Pour into 4 freezer-safe glasses; freeze for 30 minutes. Combine remaining pudding mix, strawberry ice cream and food coloring in blender; cover and blend until smooth, about 15 seconds. Pour into glasses on top of vanilla portion and serve.

★ SIMPLE INGREDIENT SWAP ★
Try swapping out ice cream for frozen custard if you're looking for a lighter treat!

Sweetheart Shakes

Mary Bettuchy, Columbia, SC

Smoked Pimento Cheese Dip

We're a military family, so we've been stationed all over the country and get to try different regional foods. Here in South Carolina, one of the most delicious things I've discovered is pimento cheese! The smoky flavor is my own spin on this classic.

Serves 8.

8-oz. pkg. smoked Cheddar cheese, shredded
8-oz. pkg. cream cheese, softened
2 4-oz. jars pimentos or roasted red peppers, drained and diced
1/4 c. mayonnaise
1/2 t. smoked salt or 1/4 t. smoke-flavored cooking sauce
1/4 t. hot pepper sauce
1/4 t. red pepper flakes
pita chips

In a food processor or blender, combine all ingredients except pita chips. Pulse until combined. If mixture is too thick, add a little more mayonnaise. If more smoky flavor or heat is desired, add more smoke or hot sauce to taste. Serve with pita chips.

Amy Hunt, Traphill, NC

Fiesta Cheese Ball

This zesty cheese ball is scrumptious with tortilla chips or crisp bread.

Serves 8 to 10.

8-oz. pkg. cream cheese, softened
3 T. sour cream
2 T. taco seasoning mix
2 to 3 green onions, finely chopped
8-oz. pkg. shredded Mexican-blend cheese

In a bowl, blend together cream cheese, sour cream, taco seasoning and onions. Form into a ball; roll ball in shredded cheese. Wrap in plastic wrap and chill for at least 2 hours before serving.

★ DOUBLE DUTY ★ Fiesta Cheese Ball also makes a wonderful sandwich spread! Try adding a thin layer to a sliced ham sandwich. Delicious as a topping for a baked potato too! Yum!

Fiesta Cheese Ball

Nancy Kremkus, Ann Arbor, MI

Pepperoni Pizza Bites

Get creative and try this recipe with other toppings too...you'll have a blast!

Makes 8 pizzas.

11-oz. tube refrigerated thin pizza crust
1/2 c. pizza sauce
8 slices pepperoni
1/2 c. shredded mozzarella cheese

Do not unroll pizza crust; cut into 8 equal pieces. Arrange dough pieces on a parchment paper-lined baking sheet, 3 inches apart. Flatten each piece of dough into a 2-inch circle. Spoon pizza sauce into the center of each; top with pepperoni and cheese. Bake at 400 degrees for 12 minutes, or until golden and cheese melts.

Allison Paschal, Royal, AR

Heavenly Warm Corn Dip

My pastor's wife makes this zesty dip for every church potluck and there is never enough of it...it disappears that fast! Serve it with scoop-type corn chips to enjoy every bit.

Makes 8 to 12 servings.

8-oz. pkg. cream cheese, softened
10-oz. can diced tomatoes with green chiles, drained
15-1/4 oz. can yellow corn, drained
15-oz. can shoepeg corn, drained
2 t. ground cumin
2 t. chili powder
1 t. garlic powder
salt to taste

Mix all ingredients together in a microwave-safe bowl. Microwave on high until heated through and cheese is melted, 2 to 3 minutes. Stir to blend; serve warm.

★ TIME-SAVING SHORTCUT ★ Frozen chopped onions are especially good time-savers for appetizers, soups and casseroles. Simply substitute the frozen onions for the same amount of fresh in your recipe.

Pepperoni Pizza Bites

Anne Richey, Syracuse, IN

Feta Cheese Ball

This is not your typical cheese ball...the taste of feta gives it Mediterranean flair!

Serves 8 to 10.

8-oz. container crumbled feta cheese
8-oz. pkg. cream cheese, softened
2 T. butter, softened
1 T. fresh dill weed, chopped
1 clove garlic, minced
assorted crackers

In a bowl, combine all ingredients except crackers. Beat with an electric mixer on low speed until well blended. Form cheese mixture into a ball and wrap in plastic wrap. Refrigerate at least 4 hours or overnight. Serve with assorted crackers.

Suzanne Erickson, Columbus, OH

Chinese Chicken Wings

Move over, hot wings. These Asian-inspired chicken wings are packed with flavor...and they're baked, not fried. Make extra, because the crowd will love them!

Makes 2 to 2-1/2 dozen.

2 to 3 lbs. chicken wings, separated
1/2 c. soy sauce
1 c. pineapple juice
1/3 c. brown sugar, packed
1 t. ground ginger
1 t. garlic salt
1/2 t. pepper
Optional: ranch salad dressing, celery sticks

Place wings in a large plastic zipping bag; set aside. Combine remaining ingredients except optional garnish. Mix well and pour over wings, turning to coat. Refrigerate overnight, turning several times. Drain wings, discarding marinade; arrange in a single layer on an ungreased jelly-roll pan. Bake at 450 degrees for 25 to 30 minutes, until golden and juices run clear when chicken is pierced with a fork. Serve with ranch dressing and celery sticks, if desired.

Chinese Chicken Wings

Staci Meyers, Cocoa, FL

Garden-Fresh Salsa

I have added corn and black beans to this salsa, too...you can't go wrong!

Makes 4 cups.

14-1/2 oz. can diced tomatoes, drained
3/4 c. green pepper, diced
1/3 c. black olives, sliced
1/3 c. Spanish onion, diced
1/3 c. red onion, diced
2 T. fresh parsley, finely chopped
2 T. garlic, minced
1 T. fresh cilantro, finely chopped
1-1/2 T. lemon juice
1 T. lime juice
2 plum tomatoes, diced
2 green onions, sliced
1 jalapeño pepper, diced
salt and pepper to taste

Combine all ingredients in a large bowl; mix well. Cover and refrigerate until ready to serve.

Pamela Geib, Cordova, MD

Crab Meltaways

Sprinkle with green onions if you'd like a little bit of color.

Makes 4 dozen.

2 8-oz. jars sharp pasteurized
    process cheese spread
1/2 c. butter
1 t. garlic salt
1 lb. crabmeat, flaked
6 English muffins, split

Combine cheese, butter and garlic salt in a saucepan over low heat until mixture is completely melted. Remove from heat; add crabmeat and mix thoroughly. Spoon mixture onto the 12 muffin halves. Arrange on a broiler pan. Broil until golden golden. Cut muffins into quarters.

★ FREEZE IT ★ Cooked bacon can easily be frozen. Wrap individual portions in paper towels to cushion, then place the towel-wrapped portions into plastic zipping bags. Freeze and store for up to 6 weeks.

Garden-Fresh Salsa

Aaron Martelli, Santa Fe, TX

Toss-It-Together Salsa

Grab a few pantry staples and whip up this last-minute appetizer...don't forget the tortilla chips!

Serves 16.

2 14-1/2 oz. cans petite-diced
   tomatoes
1 onion, diced
1 t. garlic, chopped
1/3 c. pickled jalapeños, minced
salt and pepper to taste

Combine tomatoes with juice and remaining ingredients in a small bowl; stir well. Serve immediately or, if preferred, cover and chill overnight.

Barb Stout, Delaware, OH

Minty Orange Iced Tea

A surprising, tasty twist on standard iced tea...try making this recipe with peppermint, spearmint or applemint.

Serves 6 to 8.

6 c. water
8 tea bags
1/4 c. fresh mint, chopped
3 T. sugar
2 c. orange juice
juice of 2 lemons
ice cubes

Bring water to a boil in a saucepan. Remove from heat and add tea bags, mint and sugar; steep for 20 minutes. Discard tea bags; strain out mint. Chill for at least 2 hours. Pour into a large pitcher; add juices. Serve in tall glasses over ice.

★ TIME-SAVING SHORTCUT ★ Keep kitchen scissors nearby...they make short work of snipping fresh herbs, chopping green onions or even cutting up whole tomatoes right in the can.

Toss-It-Together Salsa

Overnight Oriental Salad, Page 50

CHAPTER TWO

Soups, Salads, Sandwiches & Sides

Too-Simple Tortilla Soup, Page 92

Chicken Salad Croissant, Page 62

Beverly Bray, Huber Heights, OH

Roasted Red, Green & Yellow Peppers

These stuffed roasted peppers are as tasty as they are colorful!

Serves 6.

2 green peppers
2 red peppers
2 yellow peppers
3 T. olive oil
3 c. green onions, diced
3/4 lb. sliced mushrooms
1 T. fresh thyme, chopped
3/4 c. couscous, uncooked
6 T. water
6 plum tomatoes, chopped

Cut off the top third of each pepper and discard. Remove seeds and rinse peppers well; set aside. Heat oil in a large skillet over medium-high heat. Add onions and mushrooms; sauté for 5 minutes. Add thyme, couscous and water; blend well. Remove from heat and stir in tomatoes. Stuff peppers with couscous mixture and place in a lightly greased 13"x9" baking pan. Bake, uncovered, at 400 degrees for 35 minutes, or until peppers are tender.

Irene Robinson, Cincinnati, OH

Hot Turkey Sandwiches

Tired of Thanksgiving leftovers? Turn them into something new and tasty in a jiffy with these simple open-faced sandwiches.

Makes 4 servings.

4 slices white bread, toasted
8 thick slices deli roast turkey
3 c. prepared stuffing
1 c. turkey gravy

Place each slice of toast on a microwave-safe plate. Divide turkey, stuffing and gravy among toast slices. Microwave, uncovered, on high for 30 to 40 seconds, until heated through.

★ TAKE IT TO GO ★ Layer slices of leftover roast turkey over stuffing or mashed potatoes, ladle turkey gravy over the top and freeze... perfect for lunches or dinners on the go. Just microwave for a few minutes, until piping hot.

Roasted Red, Green & Yellow Peppers

Karen Scarbrough, Alcoa, TN

3-Bean Basil Salad

Fresh vegetables and basil from your garden will make this wonderful side dish even better!

Serves 10.

2 c. canned kidney beans, drained and rinsed
2 c. canned green beans, drained
2 c. canned chickpeas, drained and rinsed
1 red onion, sliced and separated into rings
1 carrot, peeled and grated
1/2 c. vinegar
1/2 c. oil
6 T. sugar
1 T. fresh basil, minced
3/4 t. dry mustard
salt and pepper to taste
Garnish: fresh basil leaves

Combine beans, chickpeas, onion and carrot in a large bowl. Combine remaining ingredients except garnish in a small bowl and mix well; pour over bean mixture and toss well. Cover and refrigerate overnight. Serve chilled; garnish with basil leaves.

Amy White, Nashville, OH

Grilled Garlic Burgers

Serve these with a platter of toppings like fresh romaine lettuce and slices of vine-ripened tomato, cheese, pickles and onion...let picky eaters top their own.

Makes 4 servings.

1-3/4 lbs. lean ground beef
1/2 c. onion, finely chopped
2 T. garlic, minced
2 t. salt
2 t. pepper
6 oz. fresh horseradish, peeled and shredded
1 T. oil
2 T. mustard
1/2 c. plus 2 T. catsup
2 T. sour cream
4 onion buns, split and grilled

In a large bowl, combine beef, onion, garlic, salt and pepper. Mix well and shape into 4 patties. Sprinkle with horseradish and press into patties. Coat a grill rack or large skillet with oil; heat over medium-heat. Grill patties for 4 to 5 minutes per side. While cooking, mix together mustard, catsup and sour cream. Serve burgers on grilled buns, topped with catsup mixture.

3-Bean Basil Salad

Michelle Allman, Seymour, IN

Overnight Oriental Salad

For the crunchiest salad, pour the dressing over it just before serving.

Serves 10 to 12.

3/4 c. oil
1/2 c. sugar
1/2 c. white vinegar
2 3-oz. pkgs. Oriental-flavored ramen
   noodles with seasoning packets
1 head cabbage, shredded
1 bunch green onions, chopped
1 c. sliced almonds, toasted
1 c. roasted sunflower seeds

Combine oil, sugar, vinegar and seasoning packets from noodles in a bowl and mix well; cover and refrigerate overnight. Crush noodles in a large serving bowl; add cabbage, green onions, almonds and sunflower seeds. Pour oil mixture over top and toss gently.

Debra Stephens, Owasso, OK

Mom's Pizza Subs

This recipe was created by my mother. When I was little, we had one small pizza joint in town. We loved their pizza subs, but they didn't stay in business long. When they closed, Mom studied the ingredients and we made our own at home.

Makes 8 servings.

16-oz. pkg. ground pork sausage
6-oz. can tomato paste
1/4 c. water
1 t. garlic powder
1 t. dried oregano
8 hamburger buns, split
8 slices provolone cheese
40 pepperoni slices

Brown sausage in a skillet over medium heat; drain. Stir in tomato paste, water and seasonings. Simmer for 5 minutes, or until thickened. Spoon sausage mixture onto bottoms of buns; top each with 5 pepperoni slices and one cheese slice. Add tops of buns; wrap each bun in aluminum foil. Place buns on a baking sheet. Bake at 350 degrees for 10 minutes, or until cheese melts. Unwrap carefully and serve.

★ TAKE IT TO GO ★ Mom's Pizza Subs make a delightful lunch to go! Add a side of Overnight Oriental Salad for a lunch everyone will envy!

Overnight Oriental Salad

Stephanie Mayer, Portsmouth, VA

Tomato-Basil Bisque

Such an easy, yummy way to dress up a can of tomato soup!

Serves 4.

10-oz. can fire-roasted diced
  tomatoes with garlic
10-3/4 oz. can tomato soup
1 c. milk
3 T. pesto sauce

Mix together all ingredients in a saucepan over medium-low heat. Simmer until heated through. If desired, use an immersion blender to purée soup to desired consistency.

Georgia Cooper, Helena, MT

Cranberry-Gorgonzola Green Salad

Tart dried cranberries and Gorgonzola contribute outstanding flavor to this green salad. For color and variety, add half each of an unpeeled Granny Smith apple and your favorite crisp red apple.

Serves 8.

1/3 c. oil
1/4 c. seasoned rice vinegar
3/4 t. Dijon mustard
1 clove garlic, pressed
1 small head Bibb lettuce, torn
1 small head green leaf lettuce, torn
1 apple, cored and chopped
1/3 c. coarsely chopped walnuts,
  toasted
1/3 c. sweetened dried cranberries
1/3 c. crumbled Gorgonzola cheese

Whisk together oil, vinegar, mustard and garlic in a small bowl; set aside. Just before serving, combine remaining ingredients in a large bowl. Pour dressing over salad; toss gently.

★ SIMPLE INGREDIENT SWAP ★
If you're not a fan of Gorgonzola, try swapping it out with feta or a mild goat cheese.

Cranberry-Gorgonzola Green Salad

Jennifer Steenblock, Des Moines, IA

Macaroni & Corn Bake

So delicious, you won't have any leftovers!

Serves 6 to 8.

14-3/4 oz. can creamed corn
15-1/4 oz. can corn
1 c. elbow macaroni, uncooked
1/4 c. butter, softened
1 c. pasteurized process cheese
  spread, cubed
pepper to taste

Combine all ingredients in a large bowl and mix well; spoon into a lightly greased 2-quart casserole dish. Bake, uncovered, at 350 degrees for 45 minutes.

Terri Vanden, Bosch Rock Valley, IA

French Dip au Jus

The roast in these sandwiches is melt-in-your-mouth tender, and the brown sugar added to the broth pumps up the flavor! For party-size sandwiches, substitute smaller rolls.

Serves 12.

3-1/2 to 4-lb. beef sirloin tip roast
2 c. beef broth
2/3 c. brown sugar, packed
1/4 t. seasoned salt
1 t. smoke-flavored cooking sauce
1/3 c. soy sauce
12 hoagie buns, split
12 slices Swiss cheese

Place roast in a 5-quart slow cooker. Stir together broth, brown sugar, salt and sauces; pour over roast. Cover and cook on high setting for one hour; reduce heat to low setting and cook another 9 hours. Remove roast from slow cooker, reserving broth; shred roast with 2 forks. Place shredded meat evenly on hoagie buns and top with Swiss cheese. Serve with reserved broth for dipping.

★ SIMPLE INGREDIENT SWAP ★
For a little added color and flavor, swap out plain canned corn with corn and diced peppers.

Macaroni & Corn Bake

Debbie Wilson, Weatherford, TX

Green Chile Rice

Sprinkle with diced jalapeño peppers for an extra kick!

Serves 6.

4 c. cooked rice
8-oz. pkg. shredded mozzarella
  cheese
2 c. sour cream
4-oz. can diced green chiles, drained

Combine all ingredients in an ungreased 2-quart casserole dish. Mix well. Bake, uncovered, at 400 degrees until bubbly, about 20 minutes.

Carol Mackley, Manheim, PA

Bumsteads

This is one of the Depression-era recipes my mother used to make. They were simple and inexpensive, but we thought they were really delicious... I bet you will too!

Makes 8 sandwiches.

3 eggs, hard-boiled, peeled and
  chopped
1/4 lb. white American cheese, diced
6-oz. can tuna, drained
2 T. green pepper, chopped
2 T. green olives with pimentos,
  chopped
2 T. sweet pickle relish
1/2 c. mayonnaise
8 hot dog buns, split

Combine all ingredients except buns; spoon into buns. Arrange on an aluminum foil-lined baking sheet. Bake at 350 degrees for 15 to 20 minutes, until heated through and cheese is melted.

★ SIMPLE INGREDIENT SWAP ★
If your pantry is out of tuna, try using a can of chicken instead. Just as delicious!

Green Chile Rice

Linda Day, Wall, NJ

Mom Gowdy's Ambrosia

Ambrosia looks so pretty when served in clear glass dessert cups.

Serves 8 to 10.

2 20-oz. cans pineapple chunks, drained
2 11-oz. cans mandarin oranges, drained
2 c. sour cream
2 c. mini marshmallows
1 c. sweetened flaked coconut

Mix all ingredients in a serving bowl; cover and refrigerate.

Faith Robinson, Houston, TX

Muffuletta Sandwich

This New Orleans-inspired sandwich is similar to an Italian hero-style sandwich made with a variety of meats and cheese layered on a round loaf. But what makes it distinctively a muffuletta is the olive salad.

Serves 6 to 8.

3/4 c. green olives, chopped
3/4 c. black olives, chopped
1 clove garlic, minced
1/3 c. chopped pimentos
1/4 c. fresh parsley, chopped
3/4 t. dried oregano
1/4 t. pepper
1/3 c. plus 1 T. olive oil, divided
1 round loaf Italian bread
1/2 lb. sliced honey ham
1/2 lb. sliced turkey
1/4 lb. sliced Muenster cheese
Optional: mayonnaise-type salad dressing
8 to 10 dill pickle slices

Mix olives, garlic, pimentos, parsley, seasonings and 1/3 cup oil in a small bowl; set aside. Cut loaf in half horizontally and hollow out the center. Brush cut side of bottom half with remaining oil; layer ham, turkey and cheese slices on top. Spread salad dressing between the layers, if desired. Top with pickle slices. Fill top half of loaf with the olive mixture; place bottom loaf on top and invert. Wrap tightly in plastic wrap and chill overnight. Let stand until loaf comes to room temperature; cut into wedges.

Muffuletta Sandwich

Christi Perry, Denton, TX

Cheesy Chicken & Noodle Soup

Spice up this classic by topping it with shredded Pepper Jack cheese.

Serves 6 to 8.

4 to 6 c. chicken broth
10-3/4 oz. can Cheddar cheese soup
2 to 3 c. chicken, cooked and shredded
8-oz. pkg. fine egg noodles, uncooked
1 c. milk
Optional: shredded Cheddar cheese

Combine chicken broth, soup and chicken in a large stockpot. Bring to a boil over medium heat, stirring occasionally. Add noodles. Reduce heat to medium-low; simmer until noodles are soft. Stir in milk. Spoon into bowls; sprinkle with cheese, if desired.

Sharon Ninde, Geneva, IN

Cream of Broccoli Soup

Equally good for a chilly-evening meal or a ladies' luncheon.

Serves 4.

10-3/4 oz. can cream of potato soup
10-3/4 oz. can cream of chicken soup
1-3/4 c. milk
10-oz. pkg. frozen chopped broccoli, cooked and drained
1/8 t. onion powder
1/8 t. cayenne pepper
1/2 c. shredded Cheddar cheese

In a saucepan over medium heat, stir soups and milk together until smooth. Add broccoli and seasonings. Bring to a boil, stirring frequently. Reduce heat and simmer for 5 minutes. Add cheese and stir until melted.

★ TAKE IT TO GO ★ Sandwiches are a tasty supper solution when family members will be dining at different times. Fix sandwiches ahead of time, wrap individually and refrigerate. Pop them into a toaster oven or under a broiler to heat... fresh, full of flavor and ready whenever you are!

Cheesy Chicken & Noodle Soup

Chris McCain, Mosinee, WI

Chicken Tortellini Soup

A pot of chicken soup and a cheery bouquet of posies are sure pick-me-ups for a friend who is feeling under the weather.

Serves 6.

46-oz. can chicken broth
1 lb. boneless, skinless chicken
   breasts, cooked and cubed
1 c. carrots, peeled and chopped
1/2 c. onion, chopped
1/2 c. celery, sliced
1/2 t. dried thyme
1/4 t. pepper
1 bay leaf
9-oz. pkg. cheese tortellini, uncooked

Combine all ingredients except tortellini in a stockpot; bring to a boil over medium heat. Add tortellini. Reduce heat to medium-low; cover and simmer until tortellini is tender. Discard bay leaf.

Arlene Smulski, Lyons, IL

Chicken Salad Croissant

Pick up a roasted chicken at the deli for two meals in one. Serve it hot the first night, then slice or cube the rest to become the delicious start of a sandwich, soup or salad supper the next night.

Makes 4 servings.

2 c. cooked chicken, cubed
1/3 c. celery, diced
1/4 c. raisins
1/4 c. sweetened dried cranberries
1/4 c. sliced almonds
2/3 c. mayonnaise
1 T. lemon juice
1 T. fresh parsley, minced
1 t. mustard
1/8 t. pepper
4 croissants, split in half
   horizontally
4 lettuce leaves

Combine all ingredients except croissants and lettuce leaves in a large bowl; mix well. Cover and chill for 2 to 3 hours. To assemble, place one lettuce leaf and about 3/4 cup chicken mixture on the bottom half of each croissant; top with remaining croissant halves.

Chicken Salad Croissant

Melissa Hart, Middleville, MI

Zucchini Fritters

Here's a tasty way to get your family to eat their vegetables and use the surplus zucchini from your garden.

Serves 4.

3-1/2 c. zucchini, grated
1 egg, beaten
2/3 c. shredded Cheddar cheese
2/3 c. round buttery crackers,
  crumbled
Optional: 1/2 t. seasoned salt
2 T. oil

In a large bowl, combine zucchini, egg, cheese, crackers and salt, if desired. Mix well; if mixture seems too wet, add extra crackers. Shape mixture into patties. Heat oil in a skillet over medium heat; fry patties for about 3 minutes on each side, until golden.

Crystal Bruns, Iliff, CO

Avocado Egg Salad

A fresh and delicious twist on egg salad...serve it on your favorite hearty bread.

Makes 6 servings.

6 eggs, hard-boiled, peeled and
  chopped
2 avocados, pitted, peeled and cubed
1/2 c. red onion, minced
3 T. sweet pickles, chopped
1 T. mustard
1/3 c. mayonnaise
salt and pepper to taste

Mash eggs with a fork in a bowl until crumbly. Add remaining ingredients except salt and pepper. Gently mix ingredients together until blended. Add salt and pepper to taste.

★ TIME-SAVING SHORTCUT ★ You can buy hard-boiled eggs in most grocery stores these days. So easy to whip up this Avocado Egg Salad with them!

Zucchini Fritters

Joyce Chizauskie, Vacaville, CA

Cobb Sandwiches

If you don't have time to fry bacon, bacon bits are convenient to use... just mix them with the blue cheese dressing.

Makes 2 sandwich wedges.

2 T. blue cheese salad dressing
3 slices bread, toasted
1 leaf green leaf lettuce
3 thin slices tomato
6-oz. grilled boneless, skinless
    chicken breast, sliced and divided
1 red onion, thinly sliced
3 slices avocado
3 slices bacon, crisply cooked

Spread salad dressing on one side of each slice of toasted bread. On the first slice of bread, layer lettuce, tomato and half of chicken over dressing; top with a second bread slice. Layer with onion, avocado, remaining chicken slices and bacon; top with remaining bread slice. Cut sandwich in half, securing each section with a toothpick.

Jen Chambers, Veneta, OR

Feel-Better BLT Sandwiches

My husband made these sandwiches for me when I had a bad cold and he stayed home to take care of me. They'll make anyone feel better in a hurry!

Makes 4 sandwiches.

8 slices whole-wheat bread, toasted
1 lb. thick-cut bacon, crisply cooked
    and crumbled
4 leaves Romaine lettuce
1 to 2 tomatoes, sliced
2 to 4 T. crumbled blue cheese
Garnish: mayonnaise, mustard

Layer 4 bread slices with bacon, lettuce and tomato slices. Sprinkle blue cheese over tomatoes. Spread mayonnaise and mustard on remaining 4 bread slices. Close sandwiches and serve.

★ SIMPLE INGREDIENT SWAP ★
For a real wake-you-up flavor, use creamy horseradish instead of the mayo and blue cheese.

Cobb Sandwiches

Dana Thompson, Delaware, OH

Quick & Easy Veggie Salad

A simple, healthy choice to pair with any main dish...or serve it by itself with crunchy bread.

Serves 4.

1/2 head cauliflower, chopped
1 bunch broccoli, chopped
1 tomato, chopped
1/4 red onion, sliced
3 to 4 T. Italian salad dressing

Combine cauliflower, broccoli, tomato and onion in a serving bowl. Toss with dressing to taste.

Irene Robinson, Cincinnati, OH

Fried Peppered Cabbage

This simple dish is delicious with pork chops, pot roast or chicken!

Makes 6 servings.

1/4 c. butter, sliced
1 head cabbage, coarsely chopped
salt and pepper to taste
3 T. sour cream

Melt butter in a large skillet over high heat; add cabbage. Sauté, stirring constantly, for about 2 minutes, until tender-crisp but not wilted. Season with salt and a very generous amount of pepper. Stir in sour cream. Serve immediately.

★ TIME-SAVING SHORTCUT ★ Whip this up in a jiffy using a bag of shredded cabbage!

Quick & Easy Veggie Salad

Carla Gilbert, New Haven, CT

Baby PB&J Bagel Sandwiches

These bagels put a crunchy spin on a childhood favorite.

Serves 6.

6 T. creamy peanut butter
6 mini bagels, split
6 t. strawberry or grape jelly
1 T. butter, melted

Spread peanut butter evenly on cut sides of bottom halves of bagels; spread jelly evenly on cut sides of top halves of bagels. Place top halves of bagels on bottom halves, jelly sides down. Brush bagels lightly with melted butter; cook in a preheated panini press 2 minutes or until lightly golden and grill marks appear. Serve immediately.

Fern Bruner, Phoenix, AZ

Bacon-Brown Sugar Brussels Sprouts

A delicious way to get your family to enjoy eating this leafy veggie!

Serves 6 to 8.

4 slices bacon
14-oz. can chicken broth
1 T. brown sugar, packed
1 t. salt
1-1/2 lbs. Brussels sprouts, trimmed
    and halved

Cook bacon in a Dutch oven over medium heat for 10 minutes, or until crisp. Remove bacon and drain on paper towels, reserving drippings in pan. Add chicken broth, brown sugar and salt to reserved drippings; bring to a boil. Stir in Brussels sprouts. Cover and cook for 6 to 8 minutes , until tender. Transfer to a serving bowl using a slotted spoon; sprinkle with crumbled bacon. Serve immediately.

★ SIMPLE INGREDIENT SWAP ★
In your PB&J Bagel Sandwiches, swap out the bagels for sandwich thins. Just as tasty!

Bacon-Brown Sugar Brussels Sprouts

SOUPS, SALADS, SANDWICHES & SIDES

Hollie Moots, Marysville, OH

Fried Autumn Apples

We have been taking family trips to the apple orchard for many years. This quick dish is a favorite year 'round, but is extra special made with apples we picked together.

Serves 6.

6 apples, peeled, cored and sliced
1 t. lemon juice
1/4 c. butter, sliced
1/4 c. brown sugar, packed
1 t. cinnamon
1/4 t. nutmeg
1/4 t. salt

In a bowl, toss apples with lemon juice; set aside. Melt butter in a skillet over medium-low heat. Add apples; top with brown sugar, spices and salt. Sauté, uncovered, for about 15 minutes, until apples are tender, stirring occasionally.

Dana Harpster, Kansas City, MO

Green Peas with Crispy Bacon

I've used bacon bits and even diced ham in place of the bacon in the recipe. Both worked!

Serves 6.

2 slices bacon
1 shallot, sliced
1/2 t. orange zest
1/2 c. orange juice
1/4 t. salt
1/2 t. pepper
16-oz. pkg. frozen sweet green peas, thawed
1 t. butter
1 T. fresh mint, chopped
Garnish: fresh mint sprigs

Cook bacon in a skillet over medium heat until crisp. Remove and drain on paper towels, reserving one teaspoon drippings in skillet. Crumble bacon and set aside. Sauté shallot in reserved drippings over medium-high heat for 2 minutes, or until tender. Stir in orange zest, orange juice, salt and pepper. Cook, stirring occasionally, for 5 minutes, or until liquid is reduced by half. Add peas and cook 5 more minutes; stir in butter and chopped mint. Transfer peas to a serving dish and sprinkle with crumbled bacon. Garnish as desired.

★ TIME-SAVING SHORTCUT ★ Rather
than chase little round peas around the plate, be
sure to serve this side with fluffy biscuits, or "pea
pushers," to help you get every pea on your fork.

Green Peas with Crispy Bacon

Mari Bochenek, Lacey, WA

Speedy Baked Beans

This recipe is amazing! It takes only 10 minutes in the microwave, yet the beans taste like they've been slow-baked for hours.

Serves 6 to 10.

1 lb. bacon, crisply cooked and
　　crumbled
2 15-oz. cans pork & beans
1 onion, finely chopped
1/4 c. brown sugar, packed
1/4 c. maple syrup
1/4 c. catsup
1/2 t. dry mustard
1/4 to 1/2 t. cayenne pepper

Combine all ingredients in an ungreased microwave-safe 3-quart casserole dish; mix well. Cover and microwave on high for 10 minutes.

Lori Downing, Bradenton, FL

Southwestern Layered Salad

A rainbow of colors appears in the layers of this bean and vegetable salad, so be sure to serve it in a clear glass bowl for an impressive presentation.

Serves 8.

15-oz. can black beans, drained and
　　rinsed
1/4 c. salsa
2 c. lettuce, chopped
2 tomatoes, chopped
15-1/4 oz. can corn, drained
1 green pepper, chopped
1 red onion, finely chopped
1/2 c. shredded Cheddar cheese
1/4 c. bacon bits
1 c. ranch salad dressing
Optional: tortilla chips

Mix together black beans and salsa in a small bowl. In a large serving bowl, layer bean mixture, lettuce, tomatoes, corn, green pepper, onion and cheese. Sprinkle with bacon bits; drizzle with dressing. Cover and refrigerate until ready to serve. Serve with tortilla chips, if desired.

Southwestern Layered Salad

Sam Stewart, Los Angeles, CA

Sautéed Green Beans

Simple garlic and Cajun seasoning let the garden-fresh flavor of green beans shine through.

Serves 6 to 8.

2 lbs. fresh green beans, trimmed
salt to taste
2 T. olive oil
1 red pepper, sliced
2 cloves garlic, minced
1 t. Cajun seasoning

In a large saucepan over medium-high heat, cover green beans with water; add salt to taste. Bring to a boil; boil 8 to 10 minutes, until crisp-tender. Drain and plunge into ice water to stop the cooking process; drain. Heat oil in a large skillet over medium heat; sauté red pepper for 2 minutes, or until crisp-tender. Add garlic; sauté 2 more minutes. Add green beans to skillet; sprinkle with Cajun seasoning, and cook, stirring constantly, until heated through.

Gail Peterson, Stockton, KS

Braised Beans & Tomatoes

I love this recipe! In the summer I use fresh-from-the-garden ingredients. Once my garden is tucked away for the year, then what I have frozen or canned is perfect for this recipe.

Serves 6.

2 T. butter
1 onion, thinly sliced
3 cloves garlic, minced
16-oz. pkg. frozen cut green beans
14-1/2 oz. can diced tomatoes, drained
1 to 1-1/2 c. chicken broth
salt and pepper to taste

Melt butter in a large skillet over medium heat; sauté onion. Add garlic, beans, tomatoes and enough broth to cover everything. Increase heat to high; bring to a boil. Reduce heat to low; cover and simmer for 5 to 10 minutes, until beans are tender. Uncover; simmer for 5 minutes. Season with salt and pepper.

★ FREEZE IT ★ Put a few extra burgers on the grill, then pop into buns, wrap individually and freeze. Later, just reheat in the microwave for quick meals...they'll taste freshly grilled!

Sautéed Green Beans

Alice Collins, Kansas City, MO

Roasted Corn with Rosemary Butter

The next time you fire up the grill, make room for this corn on the cob. Nothing could be better than fresh sweet corn roasted in the husk.

Serves 6.

6 ears yellow or white sweet corn, in husks
1/4 c. butter, softened
1 t. fresh rosemary, chopped

Pull back corn husks, leaving them attached. Remove and discard corn silk. Combine butter and rosemary in a small bowl; brush over corn. Pull husks over corn. Grill corn over medium-high heat (350 to 400 degrees) for about 15 minutes, turning occasionally.

Brenda Hancock, Hartford, KY

Chicken & Dumplin' Soup

Refrigerated biscuits make this ultimate comfort food ever so easy!

Serves 6 to 8.

10-3/4 oz. can cream of chicken soup
4 c. chicken broth
4 boneless, skinless chicken breasts, cooked and shredded
2 15-oz. cans mixed vegetables
12-oz. tube refrigerated biscuits, quartered
Optional: pepper to taste

Combine soup and broth in a 6-quart stockpot; bring to a boil over medium-high heat, whisking until smooth. Stir in chicken and vegetables; bring to a boil. Drop biscuit quarters into soup; cover and simmer for 15 minutes. Let soup stand for 10 minutes before serving. Sprinkle each serving with pepper, if desired.

Chicken & Dumplin' Soup

Dolores Brock, Wellton, AZ

Cheesy Potato Skins

Make a meal out of this by adding your favorite meat...barbecue pork, ham and chicken are all good choices.

Serves 4 to 8.

4 potatoes, baked and halved
1/2 c. shredded Cheddar cheese
1/2 c. shredded mozzarella cheese
2 green onions, chopped
4 t. bacon bits

Place potatoes on an ungreased baking sheet. Sprinkle with cheeses; top with onions and bacon. Heat under broiler until cheese melts.

Debby Horton, Cincinnati, OH

Easy Italian Wedding Soup

Though you probably won't see this dish on the menu at many weddings, it is a traditional Italian soup that's often served for holidays and other special events.

Serves 4.

2 14-1/2 oz. cans chicken broth
1 c. water
1 c. medium shell pasta, uncooked
16 frozen meatballs, cooked
2 c. fresh spinach, finely shredded
1 c. pizza sauce

Bring broth and one cup water to a boil in a large saucepan over medium-high heat; add pasta and meatballs. Return to a boil; cook for 7 to 9 minutes, until pasta is tender. Do not drain. Reduce heat; stir in spinach and pizza sauce. Cook for one to 2 minutes, until heated through.

★ DOUBLE DUTY ★ Crispy potato pancakes are a great way to use extra mashed potatoes. Stir an egg yolk and some minced onion into 2 cups potatoes. Form into patties and fry in butter until golden. Delicious with grilled sausage.

Cheesy Potato Skins

Karen Hibbert, Abergele, Wales

Simple Sweet Corn Soup

Fantastic for children for a warming lunchtime dish. If you prefer your onions less crunchy, sauté them in a little butter before adding to the soup. Shredded chicken can be added for a heartier soup.

Makes 4 servings.

2 c. chicken broth
1/2 t. garlic powder
1/4 t. dry mustard
salt and pepper to taste
1 c. frozen corn
14-3/4 oz. can creamed corn
2 green onions, chopped, or 2 T. dried, chopped onion
Optional: leftover mashed potatoes
saltine crackers

In a large saucepan over medium heat, stir together broth and seasonings. Add frozen corn, creamed corn and onions; stir again. Cook for several minutes, until corn is thawed. If a thicker soup is desired, stir in mashed potatoes to desired consistency. Bring to a boil. Reduce heat to medium-low; simmer for 20 minutes. Serve with crackers.

Larry Anderson, New Orleans, LA

Rice Pilaf with Carrots

This was my mother's recipe, but I added the pine nuts. I like the added crunch!

Serves 6 to 8.

1 T. oil
2 c. basmati rice, uncooked
1/4 c. onion, chopped
2 cloves garlic, minced
4 c. chicken broth
1/2 t. salt
1 c. carrots, peeled and finely chopped
1/2 c. green onions, chopped
3 T. pine nuts, toasted

Heat oil in a medium saucepan over medium-high heat. Add rice and onion; sauté for 2 minutes. Add garlic; sauté for one minute. Add chicken broth and salt; bring to a boil. Cover; reduce heat to medium-low and simmer for 7 minutes. Stir in carrots; cover and cook for 7 more minutes, or until liquid is absorbed. Remove from heat; stir in green onions and pine nuts. Let stand, covered, for 15 minutes; fluff with a fork before serving.

★ FREEZE IT ★ Rice pilaf freezes well. Make a big batch and divide individual servings into freezer containers. Easy to reheat for dinners in a hurry!

Rice Pilaf with Carrots

50 CALORIES

50 CA

Marcia Emig, Goodland, KS

Golden Homestyle Rice

This tasty rice offers a nice change of pace from potatoes.

Serves 4.

1 c. long-cooking rice, uncooked
1 T. butter
1/2 c. green onions, chopped
1/2 lb. sliced mushrooms
1-1/2 c. chicken broth
1/2 c. dry sherry or chicken broth
1 t. salt
1 t. pepper
Garnish: chopped green onions

Pour uncooked rice into a greased 11"x7" baking pan; set aside. Melt butter in a saucepan over medium heat; add green onions and sauté until soft. Add mushrooms and sauté until soft. Add chicken broth, sherry or broth, salt and pepper; bring to a boil. Remove from heat and pour over rice in baking pan. Cover and bake at 375 degrees for 25 to 30 minutes. Garnish with additional green onions.

Paula Smith, Ottawa, IL

Paula's Twice-Baked Potatoes

Top with a dollop of sour cream and a sprinkle of snipped fresh chives... heavenly!

Serves 12.

6 potatoes
1/4 c. butter, softened
1/2 c. milk
1 onion, finely chopped
6 slices bacon, crisply cooked and crumbled
1 t. salt
1/2 t. pepper
1-1/2 c. shredded Cheddar cheese, divided
Optional: sour cream, chopped fresh chives

Bake potatoes at 375 degrees for one hour, or until tender; cool. Cut each potato in half lengthwise and scoop out insides, leaving a thin shell. Mash potato pulp with butter in a bowl; add milk, onion, bacon, salt, pepper and one cup cheese. Mix well. Spoon mixture into potato shells and place on a lightly greased baking sheet. Bake at 375 degrees for 25 minutes. Top with remaining cheese; bake an additional 5 minutes, or until cheese melts. Garnish with sour cream and chopped fresh chives, if desired.

Golden Homestyle Rice

Kristie Matry, Ada, MI

White Bean Chicken Chili

Add crusty rolls and a fresh salad for a hearty meal.

Serves 4 to 6.

3 15.8-oz. cans Great Northern beans
4 boneless, skinless chicken breasts, cooked and cubed
16-oz. jar salsa
8-oz. pkg. shredded Monterey Jack cheese
8-oz. pkg. shredded Cheddar cheese

Combine all ingredients in a stockpot. Cook over low heat until cheeses melt, stirring often. Stir in up to one cup water for desired consistency; heat until warmed through.

Donna Meyer, Fargo, ND

Sweet Onion Side Dish

Onion-lovers will rave over this tasty dish that's cooked in the microwave in minutes.

Serves 2.

2 sweet onions, peeled
2 cubes beef bouillon
1 T. butter
Optional: fresh parsley, pepper

Cut a thin slice from the top and bottom of each onion. Scoop out a one-inch-deep hole from the top of each onion. Place onions, top sides up, in a 2-quart microwave-safe dish with a lid. Place one bouillon cube and 1/2 tablespoon butter in each onion. Microwave, covered, on high for 8 to 10 minutes, until onion is tender. Garnish with fresh parsley and pepper, if desired.

White Bean Chicken Chili

Marcia Frahm, Urbandale, IA

Skinny Salsa Joes

Serve on toasty sandwich buns for a taste that can't be beat!

Serves 4.

1 lb. ground beef
1/2 c. salsa
8-oz. can tomato sauce
1 T. brown sugar, packed
4 sandwich buns, split

Brown beef in a large skillet over medium heat; drain. Stir in remaining ingredients except buns. Bring to a boil; reduce heat to medium-low and simmer for 10 to 15 minutes. To serve, spoon onto buns.

Julie Saifullah, Lexington, KY

Corn, Black Bean & Avocado Salad

Paired with a lime vinaigrette, this quick & easy Southwestern-inspired vegetarian salad is the perfect chilled salad for warm days.

Serves 4 to 6.

15-oz. can black beans, drained and rinsed
15-oz. can shoepeg corn, drained
1 avocado, halved, pitted and diced
6 green onions, thinly sliced
2 c. tomatoes, chopped, or grape tomatoes, halved
Optional: 1/2 c. chopped fresh cilantro
1/2 c. lime vinaigrette salad dressing
salt and pepper to taste

In a large bowl, combine beans, corn, avocado, onions, tomatoes and cilantro, if using. Pour vinaigrette over salad. Add salt and pepper to taste. Stir salad to coat vegetables with dressing; cover and chill until serving.

★ SIMPLE INGREDIENT SWAP ★ Mmm... mashed potatoes are the ultimate comfort food. Simmer potatoes in chicken broth instead of water for delicious flavor.

Skinny Salsa Joes

Betty Kidd, Washington, DC

Monster Meatball Sandwiches

Your family will love these dinner roll meatball sandwiches...perfect for game days.

Makes 16.

32 frozen bite-size meatballs
9-oz. jar mango chutney
1 c. chicken broth
16 dinner rolls
Garnish: sweet-hot pickle sandwich
    relish

Stir together meatballs, chutney and chicken broth in a saucepan. Bring to a boil over medium-high heat. Reduce heat to low and simmer, stirring occasionally, for 25 to 30 minutes. Cut rolls vertically through top, cutting to, but not through, the bottom. Place 2 meatballs in each roll. Top with relish.

Beth Childers, Urbana, OH

Spring Spinach Sauté

This delicious vegetarian dish is also great with pork chops.

Serves 4.

1 to 2 cloves garlic, minced
2 T. olive oil
6-oz. pkg. baby spinach
1/2 c. crumbled feta cheese
1/4 c. slivered almonds

In a skillet over medium heat, sauté garlic in hot oil until golden. Add spinach; cook and stir until crisp-tender. Stir in feta cheese and almonds; heat through.

★ TIME-SAVING SHORTCUT ★
Apples, bananas and tomatoes ripen quickly if placed overnight in a brown paper bag.

Monster Meatball Sandwiches

Edward Kielar, Whitehouse, OH

Bacon Quesadillas

These savory snacks have zing...
such flavor!

Serves 4.

1 c. shredded Colby Jack cheese
1/4 c. bacon bits
1/4 c. green onions, thinly sliced
Optional: 4-1/2 oz. can diced green
    chiles, 1/4 c. chopped red or green
    pepper
4 6-inch flour tortillas
Garnish: sour cream, salsa

Combine cheese, bacon bits and onion
in a bowl; add chiles and peppers, if
desired. Sprinkle mixture equally
over one half of each tortilla. Fold
tortillas in half; press lightly to seal
edges. Arrange on a lightly greased
baking sheet. Bake at 400 degrees
for 8 to 10 minutes, until edges are
lightly golden. Top with a dollop of
sour cream and salsa.

Paulette Cunningham, Lompoc, CA

Too-Simple Tortilla Soup

Top this soup with a couple of slices
of avocado, fresh cilantro or a dollop
of sour cream.

Serves 6 to 8.

2 14-1/2 oz. cans chicken broth
2 10-oz. cans chicken, drained
2 15-oz. cans white hominy, drained
16-oz. jar salsa
1 T. ground cumin

Combine all ingredients in a
stockpot; bring to a boil over
medium-high heat. Reduce heat
to medium-low; cook until
warmed through.

★ SIMPLE INGREDIENT SWAP ★
**Spice up frozen French fries! Simply
spritz with olive oil and sprinkle with chili
powder before popping them in the oven.**

Bacon Quesadillas

Easy Spaghetti & Meatballs, Page 100

CHAPTER THREE

Delicious Dinners

Family Favorite Chili Mac, Page 104

Easy Cheesy Manicotti, Page 126

Vickie, Gooseberry Patch

Lime & Ginger Grilled Salmon

I've tried this recipe using lemon zest too...it's delicious!

Serves 4.

2-lb. salmon fillet
2 T. fresh ginger, peeled and minced
2 T. lime zest
1/2 t. salt
1/2 t. pepper
2 T. butter, melted, or olive oil
1/2 t. lime juice

Preheat grill to medium-high heat (350 to 400 degrees). Sprinkle salmon with ginger, lime zest, salt and pepper. Combine butter or olive oil and lime juice in a small bowl; brush salmon with mixture. Grill for about 5 minutes on each side, until salmon flakes easily with a fork.

Amy Hunt, Traphill, NC

Oktoberfest Pie

A wonderful easy meal to share after a day at the pumpkin patch. Add some pickled beets and hot rolls on the side...your family may just take you out for dessert!

Makes 6 servings.

14-oz. pkg. Kielbasa turkey sausage, cut into 1/2-inch pieces
14-oz. can sauerkraut, drained
1 c. shredded Swiss cheese
3/4 c. low-fat biscuit baking mix
1/2 c. skim milk
1/2 c. non-alcoholic beer
2 eggs, beaten

Spray a 9" glass pie plate with non-stick vegetable spray. Layer Kielbasa, sauerkraut and cheese in pie plate; set aside. In a bowl, stir together remaining ingredients until well blended; pour over cheese. Bake, uncovered, at 400 degrees for about 35 minutes. Let stand several minutes; cut into wedges.

★ DOUBLE DUTY ★ Extra cooked pasta doesn't need to go to waste. Toss with oil, wrap tightly and refrigerate up to 4 days. To serve, place in a metal colander, dip into boiling water for one minute and drain...as good as fresh-cooked!

Lime & Ginger Grilled Salmon

Heather Riley, Johnston, IA

Baked Barbecue Chicken

Bacon and mushrooms transform ordinary barbecue chicken.

Serves 4.

4 boneless, skinless chicken breasts
1 c. all-purpose flour
6 to 7 slices bacon
8-oz. can mushroom stems & pieces, drained
1-1/2 c. barbecue sauce

Coat chicken breasts in flour; arrange in a lightly greased 13"x9" baking pan. Lay bacon slices across chicken. Bake, uncovered, at 400 degrees for 45 minutes. Drain; top with mushroom pieces and barbecue sauce. Bake 15 minutes longer.

Leea Mercer, League City, TX

Leea's Quick Spaghetti

My kids love this...it's delicious and very budget-friendly too!

Serves 4.

7-oz. pkg. spaghetti, uncooked
1 lb. ground beef
1/2 c. onion, diced
salt and pepper to taste
2 8-oz. cans tomato sauce
6-oz. can tomato paste
3 cloves garlic, minced
2 to 3 T. dried basil
1 to 2 t. dried oregano

Cook spaghetti according to package directions; drain. Meanwhile, brown beef and onion in a skillet over medium heat; drain. Add salt and pepper; stir in tomato sauce, tomato paste, garlic and seasonings. If too thick, add a little water. Reduce heat to low. Simmer for 20 to 30 minutes, stirring occasionally. Serve sauce over spaghetti.

Baked Barbecue Chicken

Lisa Arning, Garden City, NY

Poppy's Onion Pizza

For a light vegetarian dinner, this pizza is the best choice.

Serves 8.

3 T. olive oil, divided
10-inch refrigerated pizza crust
2 onions, diced
garlic powder and paprika to taste
Optional: salt and pepper to taste

Lightly coat a pizza pan with one tablespoon olive oil; place pizza dough into pan. Coat dough with one tablespoon oil; set aside. In a saucepan over medium heat, sauté onions in remaining oil until golden. Spread onions evenly over the pizza dough, lightly pressing down. Sprinkle with desired seasonings. Bake at 425 degrees for 20 minutes, or until golden. Cut into wedges.

Stephanie Whisenhunt, Birmingham, AL

Easy Spaghetti & Meatballs

One taste of this homemade sauce, and family & friends will think that it has simmered all day long. You don't have to share that it only took 20 minutes!

Serves 4 to 6.

10-oz. pkg. spaghetti, uncooked
24 frozen Italian-style meatballs, thawed
2 14-1/2 oz. cans Italian-style diced tomatoes
2 6-oz. cans tomato paste
1/2 c. water
2 t. Italian seasoning
2 t. sugar
Optional: grated Parmesan cheese

Cook pasta according to package directions; drain and keep warm. Meanwhile, add meatballs, tomatoes with juice and remaining ingredients except Parmesan cheese to a Dutch oven. Cook over medium heat for 20 minutes, stirring occasionally, until hot and bubbly. Serve meatballs and sauce over hot cooked pasta. Sprinkle with Parmesan cheese, if desired.

★ TIME-SAVING SHORTCUT ★ Move
frozen meat into the fridge to thaw overnight.
Fresh meat can be sliced or chopped ahead
of time.

Easy Spaghetti & Meatballs

Carole Larkins, Elmendorf AFB, AK

Fettuccine with Smoked Salmon

I like to serve this spooned into a serving bowl ringed with fresh lettuce leaves.

Serves 4 to 6.

8-oz. pkg. fettuccine pasta, uncooked
1 lb. asparagus, cut into 1/2-inch
   pieces
1 c. whipping cream
2 T. fresh dill, chopped
1 T. prepared horseradish
1/4 lb. smoked salmon, cut into
   1/2-inch pieces
1/2 t. salt
1/4 t. pepper
juice of 1/2 lemon

Cook pasta according to package directions; add asparagus during last 3 minutes of cooking time. Drain and set aside. Combine cream, dill and horseradish in a skillet over low heat; cook and stir for one minute or until hot. Add pasta mixture, tossing to mix. Gently toss in salmon; add salt and pepper. Drizzle lemon juice over top.

Mary Ludemann, Bronx, NY

American Chop Suey

My grandmother used to make this simple dish for my mom, and Mom made it for my brother and me. I always asked her to make this for my birthday instead of something fancier! Now my two kids love it...my 8-year-old always gets excited when I make it.

Serves 6.

16-oz. pkg. elbow macaroni, uncooked
1 lb. ground beef
15-oz. can tomato sauce
2 10-3/4 oz. cans tomato soup

Cook macaroni according to package directions; drain and return to cooking pot. Meanwhile, brown beef in a skillet over medium heat; drain. Add beef and remaining ingredients to macaroni. Cook over medium heat, stirring occasionally, until heated through.

★ TIME-SAVING SHORTCUT ★ Making a big batch of meatballs? Brown them the easy way...simply place meatballs in a roasting pan and bake for 15 to 20 minutes at 375 degrees.

Fettuccine with Smoked Salmon

Stephanie McNealy, Talala, OK

Family Favorite Chili Mac

Kids love this quick & easy dinner. Serve with a tossed salad and cornbread sticks.

Serves 7 to 9.

2 7-1/4 oz. pkgs. macaroni & cheese mix, uncooked
10-oz. can diced tomatoes with green chiles
1 to 2 lbs. ground beef
1-1/4 oz. pkg. taco seasoning mix
chili powder, salt and pepper to taste

Prepare macaroni & cheese according to package directions. Stir in tomatoes; set aside. Brown beef in a skillet over medium heat; drain and stir in taco seasoning. Stir beef mixture into macaroni mixture. Add seasonings as desired; heat through.

Linda Lamb, Round Rock, TX

Poor Man's Cordon Bleu

A quick & easy variation on a classic.

Serves 4.

16 slices deli turkey
8 slices deli ham
16 slices Swiss cheese
1/2 c. water
2 c. Italian-flavored dry bread crumbs, divided

For each turkey roll, lay out 2 turkey slices, overlapping ends by 2 to 3 inches. Add a ham slice, centered on turkey slices. Place 2 cheese slices on top, with ends barely touching. Roll up, starting on one short side. Repeat with remaining ingredients to make 8 rolls. Dip rolls into water to moisten. Coat in bread crumbs, reserving 1/4 cup bread crumbs for topping. Place rolls seam-side down in a greased 13"x9" baking pan. Sprinkle reserved crumbs on top. Bake, uncovered, at 350 degrees for 15 to 20 minutes, until lightly golden and cheese is melted.

★ TIME-SAVING SHORTCUT ★ Buy precut veggies like broccoli flowerets, green pepper strips and sliced onion from the supermarket's salad bar. Bags of shredded coleslaw mix are time-savers too.

Family Favorite Chili Mac

Wayne Smith, Wesson, MS

Savory Cranberry Chicken

Perfect for a holiday feast...pair it with homemade stuffing.

Serves 6.

6 boneless, skinless chicken breasts
16-oz. can whole-berry cranberry
   sauce
8-oz. bottle French salad dressing
1-1/2 oz. pkg. onion soup mix

Arrange chicken in a lightly greased 13"x9" baking pan; set aside. Combine remaining ingredients; mix well and spoon over chicken. Cover with aluminum foil. Bake at 350 degrees for one hour, or until chicken juices run clear.

LaShelle Brown, Mulvane, KS

Idaho Tacos

This is a tasty quick & easy meal to toss together on a busy day. If time is short, you can bake the potatoes in the microwave while you are making the beef mixture to go on top.

Makes 4 servings.

4 russet potatoes, baked
1 lb. ground beef
1-1/4 oz. pkg. taco seasoning mix
1/2 c. water
1 c. shredded Cheddar cheese
Garnish: sliced green onions
Optional: salsa

With a sharp knife, cut an X in the top of each warm potato; fluff pulp with a fork and set aside. Brown beef in a skillet over medium heat; drain. Stir in seasoning mix and water; bring to a boil. Simmer over low heat for 5 to 7 minutes, stirring occasionally. To serve, top potatoes with beef mixture, cheese, green onions and salsa, if desired.

★ DOUBLE DUTY ★ Baked ham and roast turkey breast are holiday favorites...why not enjoy them year 'round? Sliced or cubed, they're delicious in noodle bakes, hearty sandwiches and oh-so-many other ways.

Savory Cranberry Chicken

Dianne Young, South Jordan, UT

Beef & Cheddar Quiche

So yummy topped with sour cream or your favorite salsa.

Serves 8.

1 c. ground beef
3 eggs, beaten
1 c. whipping cream
1 c. shredded Cheddar cheese
9-inch pie crust

Brown beef in a skillet over medium heat; drain. Add remaining ingredients except pie crust; mix well and spread in pie crust. Bake at 450 degrees for 15 minutes; lower oven temperature to 350 degrees and continue baking for 15 minutes.

Evelyn Bennett, Salt Lake City, UT

Easy Eggs Benedict

This version is easy because the sauce is a simple blend of mayonnaise, lemon juice and whipping cream that takes about 5 quick minutes to make!

Serves 4 to 8.

8 eggs
1/4 c. whipping cream
3/4 c. mayonnaise
1/4 t. salt
1 t. lemon zest
1 T. lemon juice
4 English muffins, split and toasted
butter to taste
8 slices Canadian bacon or deli ham

Lightly grease a large skillet; add water to a depth of 2 inches. Bring to a boil; reduce heat, maintaining a light simmer. Working in batches to poach 4 eggs at a time, break eggs, one at a time, into a cup; slip egg into water, holding cup close to water. Simmer for 5 minutes or until done. Remove eggs with a slotted spoon; set aside. In a deep bowl, beat whipping cream with an electric mixer on high speed until soft peaks form; set aside. Combine mayonnaise and salt in a small saucepan. Cook over low heat, stirring constantly, for 3 minutes. Stir in whipped cream, lemon zest and lemon juice; remove from heat and keep warm. Spread split sides of muffin halves with butter. Arrange bacon on muffin halves; top each bacon slice with a poached egg. Spoon sauce over eggs.

Easy Eggs Benedict

Melody Taynor, Everett, WA

Lemony Pork Piccata

Serve over quick-cooking angel hair pasta to enjoy every drop of the lemony sauce.

Serves 4.

1-lb. pork tenderloin, sliced into
   8 portions
2 t. lemon-pepper seasoning
3 T. all-purpose flour
2 T. butter, divided
1/4 c. dry sherry or chicken broth
1/4 c. lemon juice
1/4 c. capers
4 to 6 thin slices lemon

Pound pork slices to 1/8-inch thickness, using a meat mallet or rolling pin. Lightly sprinkle pork with seasoning and flour. Melt one tablespoon butter in a large skillet over medium-high heat. Add half of pork and sauté for 2 to 3 minutes on each side, until golden, turning once. Remove pork to a serving plate; set aside. Repeat with remaining butter and pork. Add sherry or chicken broth, lemon juice, capers and lemon slices to skillet. Cook for 2 minutes or until slightly thickened, scraping up browned bits. Add pork and heat through.

LaShelle Brown, Mulvane, KS

Cashew Nut Chicken

Your family will love this easy, delicious recipe. The longer the chicken marinates, the better it will taste, so feel free to tuck it in the fridge the night before.

Makes 4 servings.

4 boneless, skinless chicken breasts,
   cut into 1-inch cubes
soy sauce to taste
1/2 to 1 bunch green onions, chopped
2 T. oil
1/2 c. cashew halves or pieces
cooked rice

Place chicken in a glass dish; add soy sauce to taste. Cover and let stand at least 15 minutes to overnight (refrigerate if more than one hour). Heat oil in a wok or skillet over medium-high heat. Drain chicken and add along with green onions; cook and stir until chicken is almost done. Add cashews; continue cooking for several minutes, until cashews soften. To serve, spoon over cooked rice.

★ DOUBLE DUTY ★ Extra ground beef is tasty in so many easy recipes...tacos, chili and casseroles to name a few! Brown 3 or 4 pounds at a time, divide it into plastic zipping bags and refrigerate or freeze for future use.

Lemony Pork Piccata

Vickie, Gooseberry Patch

Fresh Tomato & Basil Linguine

One of my favorite quick & easy dinners!

Serves 4 to 6.

16-oz. pkg. linguine pasta, uncooked
1-1/2 lbs. tomatoes, finely chopped
3 cloves garlic, minced
1 red pepper, chopped
1 bunch fresh basil, torn
1/2 c. olive oil
1 t. salt
1/4 t. pepper
Garnish: grated Parmesan cheese

Cook pasta according to package directions; drain. Meanwhile, stir together tomatoes, garlic, red pepper and basil in a large bowl; drizzle with oil. Sprinkle with salt and pepper; mix well and toss with hot cooked linguine. Sprinkle with Parmesan cheese, if desired.

Sonya Collett, Sioux City, IA

Zesty Picante Chicken

Spice up suppertime with yummy southwestern-style chicken breasts, made in the slow cooker.

Serves 4.

4 boneless, skinless chicken breasts
16-oz. jar picante sauce
15-1/2 oz. can black beans, drained
   and rinsed
4 slices American cheese
2-1/4 c. cooked rice
Optional: sliced green onions

Place chicken in a 5-quart slow cooker; top with picante sauce and beans. Cover and cook on high setting for 3 hours, or until juices run clear when chicken is pierced with a fork. Top with cheese slices; cover and let stand until melted. To serve, arrange chicken on rice; spoon sauce mixture over all. Garnish with green onions, if desired.

Zesty Picante Chicken

Shelley Wellington, Dyersburg, TN

3-Ingredient Sausage Squares

This recipe can easily be halved and baked in an 8"x8" baking pan.

Serves 12.

2 lbs. ground pork sausage
2 8-oz. pkgs. cream cheese, softened
2 8-oz. tubes refrigerated crescent rolls

Brown sausage in a skillet over medium heat; drain. Add cream cheese, stirring until melted and well blended; remove from heat and set aside. Press dough from one tube crescent rolls into a greased 13"x9" baking pan, being sure to cover bottom and part of the way up sides of dish; press seams together. Spoon sausage mixture over top; set aside. Roll remaining crescent roll dough into a 13"x9" rectangle; layer over sausage mixture. Bake, uncovered, at 350 degrees for 15 to 20 minutes, until golden. Cut into squares to serve.

Shirley Howie, Foxboro, MA

Easy Chicken & Tomato Rice

I like to use rotisserie chicken in this recipe, which makes it delicious and ready to serve in a jiffy.

Serves 4.

10-1/2 oz. can chicken broth
14-1/2 oz. can stewed tomatoes
1 t. garlic powder
1 t. dried basil
2 c. cooked chicken, cubed
1-1/2 c. instant rice, uncooked
1 c. peas

In a saucepan over high heat, combine broth, tomatoes with juice and seasonings. Bring to a boil. Add chicken, uncooked rice and peas; return to a boil. Remove from heat. Cover and let stand for 5 minutes, or until most of the liquid is absorbed. Fluff rice with a fork before serving.

★ TIME-SAVING SHORTCUT ★

Whenever you make a favorite recipe, why not cook up extra meat, pasta or rice and refrigerate it? Later, the reserved ingredient will become the start of a different family-pleasing dish.

3-Ingredient Sausage Squares

Kathy Wood, La Crescenta, CA

Oven-Baked Chicken Fingers

Heating your baking sheet prior to cooking ensures crispier results for your chicken fingers. Serve them with ranch dressing, barbecue sauce or honey mustard for dipping.

Serves 6.

1 c. Italian-flavored dry bread crumbs
2 T. grated Parmesan cheese
1/4 c. oil
1 clove garlic, minced
6 boneless, skinless chicken breasts

Preheat oven to 425 degrees. Heat a large baking sheet in the oven for 5 minutes. Meanwhile, combine bread crumbs and cheese in a shallow dish; set aside. Combine oil and garlic in a small bowl; set aside. Place chicken between 2 sheets of heavy-duty plastic wrap. Flatten chicken to 1/2-inch thickness, using a meat mallet or rolling pin; cut into one-inch-wide strips. Dip strips into oil mixture; coat with crumb mixture. Coat preheated baking sheet with non-stick vegetable spray and arrange chicken on prepared baking sheet. Bake at 425 degrees for 12 to 14 minutes, turning after 10 minutes, until golden and chicken is no longer pink in the center.

Betsy Banner, Worthington, OH

Speedy Skillet Chops

Perfect with mashed potatoes!

Makes 2 to 4 servings.

1 to 2 T. olive oil
4 boneless pork chops
1/2 t. garlic powder
1 t. paprika
salt and pepper to taste

In a skillet over medium heat, heat oil. Add pork chops and seasonings. Cook for about 10 minutes on each side, until pork chops are cooked through.

★ DOUBLE DUTY ★ Fill a big shaker with a favorite all-purpose spice mixture...keep it by the stove for a dash of flavor on meats and veggies as they cook.

Oven-Baked Chicken Fingers

Margaret Vinci, Pasadena, CA

Momma's Divine Divan

Choose rotisserie chicken from your supermarket deli to add more flavor to this family favorite. Generally, one rotisserie chicken will yield 3 cups of chopped meat, so you'll need 2 rotisserie chickens to get the 4 to 5 cups needed for this recipe. Add cooked rice, and you have a complete meal!

Serves 8 to 10.

1/2 lb. broccoli flowerets, cooked
4 to 5 boneless, skinless chicken
  breasts, cooked and cubed
salt to taste
1 c. seasoned dry bread crumbs
1 T. butter, melted
10-3/4 oz. can cream of chicken soup
1/2 c. mayonnaise
1 t. curry powder
1/2 t. lemon juice
1 c. shredded Cheddar cheese

Arrange broccoli in a lightly greased 13"x9" baking pan. Sprinkle chicken with salt to taste; place on top of broccoli and set aside. Toss together bread crumbs and butter; set aside. Combine soup, mayonnaise, curry powder and lemon juice in a separate bowl; spread over chicken and broccoli. Top with cheese; sprinkle with bread crumb mixture. Bake, uncovered, at 350 degrees for 25 minutes, or until hot and bubbly. Serves 8 to 10.

Tammy Steinert, Hoisington, KS

Salsa Mac & Cheese

A super meal for hurry-up nights!

Serves 4.

7-1/4 oz. pkg. macaroni & cheese mix
1/2 lb. ground beef, browned
1/2 c. salsa

Prepare macaroni & cheese according to package directions. Add beef and salsa to same saucepan. Stir well and heat through over low heat.

Momma's Divine Divan

Diana Duff, Cypress, CA

Chicken Chimies

Add a bit of heat to this Mexican favorite by using Pepper Jack cheese in place of Monterey Jack.

Serves 6 to 8.

2 boneless, skinless chicken breasts, cooked and shredded
salt, pepper and garlic salt to taste
1 T. butter
10 8-inch flour tortillas
8-oz. pkg. shredded Monterey Jack cheese
6 green onions, diced
1 T. oil
Garnish: sour cream, guacamole, salsa
Optional: lettuce leaves

Season chicken with salt, pepper and garlic salt to taste. Heat butter in a skillet over medium heat; add chicken and sauté about 3 minutes, until heated through. Spoon chicken evenly onto tortillas. Top with cheese and green onions; fold up sides and roll up, burrito-style. Heat oil in a large skillet over medium-high heat. Add rolled-up tortillas and sauté until golden. Serve with your choice of toppings and over lettuce leaves, if desired.

Gladys Brehm, Quakertown, PA

Pork Cacciatore

This recipe was handed down in my family. It's quick and delicious.

Serves 4 to 5.

1 T. olive oil
1 onion, chopped
4-oz. can sliced mushrooms, drained
1 clove garlic, minced
10-oz. can diced tomatoes
1 lb. boneless pork loin, cut into bite-size pieces
1 t. Italian seasoning
1/2 t. salt
1/2 t. sugar
cooked white or brown rice

Heat oil in a skillet over medium heat. Add onion, mushrooms and garlic; sauté for 3 minutes, or until slightly softened. Stir in tomatoes with juice, pork, seasonings and sugar. Cover and simmer for 10 minutes, or until pork is no longer pink in the center. To serve, spoon pork mixture over cooked rice.

Chicken Chimies

Donna Riggins, Albertville, AL

Old-Fashioned Chicken Pot Pie

This makes two savory pies...share one with a neighbor or freeze it to use later.

Makes 2 pies, 6 servings each.

4 9-inch frozen pie crusts, thawed
  and divided
5 to 6 boneless, skinless chicken
  breasts, cooked and chopped
1 onion, chopped
10-3/4 oz. can cream of chicken soup
10-3/4 oz. can cream of mushroom
  soup
8-oz. container sour cream
salt and pepper to taste

Line two 9" pie plates with one crust each; set aside. Combine remaining ingredients in a large bowl; mix well. Divide mixture between pie plates; top with remaining crusts. Crimp crusts to seal and cut several slits in top. Bake at 350 degrees for 35 to 45 minutes, until bubbly and crusts are golden.

Bobbi Scheafnocker, Grove City, PA

Garlicky Shrimp & Pasta

My husband and I often use this recipe as our "go-to" dinner when we are out of ideas or short on time and energy.

Makes 2 to 3 servings.

2 to 3 cloves garlic, minced
5 T. butter
1/2 lb. cooked peeled shrimp, thawed
  if frozen
cooked angel hair pasta
Garnish: Italian-seasoned dry bread
  crumbs

In a skillet over medium heat, sauté garlic in butter until just heated through. Add shrimp and heat through. Serve over cooked pasta; garnish with bread crumbs.

★ TIME-SAVING SHORTCUT ★ **Roll up sets of silverware in cloth napkins as you take it from the dishwasher...all ready for next mealtime!**

Old-Fashioned Chicken Pot Pie

Lynn Ruble, Decatur, IN

Honey Chicken Stir-Fry

Measure out the seasonings before you begin to stir-fry...you'll find this dish comes together very quickly.

Serves 4 to 6.

4 T. honey, divided
1/3 c. plus 1 T. water, divided
1 egg, beaten
1 t. Worcestershire sauce
1/2 t. dried thyme
1/4 t. lemon-pepper seasoning
1/4 t. garlic powder
1/8 t. dried oregano
1/8 t. dried marjoram
2 lbs. boneless, skinless chicken strips, cut into cubes
2 T. oil
1 T. cornstarch
14-oz. pkg. frozen stir-fry vegetables
1/4 t. salt
cooked rice

Combine 2 tablespoons honey, 1/3 cup water, egg, Worcestershire sauce and seasonings. Add chicken and stir to coat; set aside. Heat oil in a wok or large skillet over medium-high heat. Add chicken a few pieces at a time; cook and stir until golden. Remove chicken from wok; keep warm. Mix cornstarch with remaining honey and water; set aside. Add vegetables to wok; sprinkle with salt. Cook over medium heat until vegetables begin to thaw; drizzle with cornstarch mixture. Continue cooking until vegetables are tender; stir in chicken and heat through. Serve with rice.

Zoe Bennett, Columbia, SC

Simple Garlic Chicken

Just five ingredients and twenty minutes from start to finish...you just can't go wrong with this recipe! It's really delicious served with rice and a crisp garden salad.

Serves 4.

3 T. butter
4 boneless, skinless chicken breasts
2 t. garlic powder
1 t. onion powder
1 t. seasoned salt

Melt butter in a large skillet over medium-high heat. Add chicken and sprinkle with seasonings. Sauté about 10 to 15 minutes on each side, until chicken is cooked through and juices run clear.

★ TIME-SAVING SHORTCUT ★ Pick up some paper plates and cups in seasonal designs...they'll make dinner fun even when you're in a hurry and clean-up will be a breeze.

Honey Chicken Stir-Fry

Valerie Neeley, Robinson, IL

Zesty Pizza Casserole

Add your favorite pizza toppings to this easy casserole.

Serves 4 to 6.

1 lb. ground beef
1/2 c. onion, chopped
1/2 c. green pepper, chopped
2 c. cooked elbow macaroni
2 15-oz. cans pizza sauce
4-oz. can sliced mushrooms, drained
4-oz. pkg. sliced pepperoni
1/2 t. dried oregano
1/2 t. garlic powder
1/2 t. dried basil
1/2 t. salt
3/4 c. shredded mozzarella cheese
Garnish: sliced fresh basil

Brown beef with onion and green pepper in a large skillet over medium heat. Drain; stir in remaining ingredients except cheese and garnish. Transfer to a lightly greased 2-quart casserole dish; sprinkle with cheese. Bake, uncovered, at 350 degrees for 30 to 45 minutes, until hot and bubbly. Garnish with basil.

Robin Argyle, Kalkaska, MI

Easy Cheesy Manicotti

This dish freezes well. Why not make 2 and freeze one for another night?

Serves 6.

12-oz. pkg. manicotti shells, uncooked
1 T. olive oil
1-1/2 t. salt, divided
8-oz. pkg. cream cheese, softened
2 c. cottage cheese
12-oz. pkg. shredded Monterey Jack cheese
12-oz. pkg. shredded mozzarella cheese, divided
1 egg, beaten
1 T. fresh parsley, chopped
1 clove garlic, minced
24-oz. jar spaghetti sauce, divided
Optional: chopped fresh parsley

Cook manicotti according to package directions, adding oil and one teaspoon salt; drain and set aside. Meanwhile, combine cream cheese, cottage cheese, Monterey Jack cheese, 2/3 of mozzarella cheese, egg, parsley, garlic and remaining salt; set aside. Spread a thin layer of spaghetti sauce in the bottom of an ungreased 13"x9" baking pan. Spoon cheese filling into each manicotti, filling 3/4 full; arrange on top of sauce. Spoon remaining sauce over manicotti. Bake, uncovered, at 350 degrees for 30 to 45 minutes. Top with remaining mozzarella cheese 10 minutes before done. Let stand minutes before serving. Garnish with additional parsley, if desired.

Easy Cheesy Manicotti

Rebecca Brock, Muskogee, OK

Beef & Bean Burritos

I've been serving these burritos for years at get-togethers and they've become a family favorite. Add warm cornbread or crunchy corn chips and dinner is ready!

Makes 12 servings.

1 lb. ground beef
1 onion, chopped
16-oz. can refried beans
1-1/4 oz. pkg. taco seasoning mix
1/2 c. water
12 10-inch flour tortillas
8-oz. jar taco sauce
16-oz. jar picante sauce
1-1/2 c. favorite shredded cheese

Brown beef and onion in a skillet over medium heat; drain. Add beans, seasoning mix and water to skillet; simmer until heated through. Place tortillas between dampened paper towels. Microwave on high setting for 30 to 60 seconds, until warm. Divide beef mixture evenly among tortillas; roll up. Place burritos seam-side down in a lightly greased 13"x9" baking pan. Mix sauces and pour evenly over burritos. Microwave, uncovered, on high for about 10 minutes, until hot and bubbly. Top with cheese; let stand until cheese melts.

Jerry Lyttle, St. Clair Shores, MI

Beef Fajita Skewers

Serve with warmed flour tortillas, sour cream and salsa...a clever new way to enjoy a Mexican restaurant favorite.

Makes 4 to 6 servings.

1 lb. boneless beef top sirloin, sliced
    into 1-inch cubes
8 wooden skewers, soaked in water
1 green pepper, cut into wedges
1 red or yellow pepper, cut into
    wedges
2 onions, cut into wedges
3 T. lime juice
1/3 c. Italian salad dressing
salt to taste

Thread beef cubes onto 4 skewers; thread peppers and onions onto remaining skewers. Combine lime juice and salad dressing; brush over skewers. Grill over hot coals or on a medium-hot grill, turning occasionally, 7 to 9 minutes for beef and 12 to 15 minutes for vegetables. Sprinkle with salt to taste.

Beef Fajita Skewers

Marie Buche, Yakima, WA

Hamburger Pie

With a family of six on a ministry budget, this easy, affordable recipe became the first dinner I taught my three daughters and my son to prepare. Even the leftovers are tasty. This is also my most-requested church potluck recipe. Serve with cinnamon-spiced applesauce for a wonderful family dinner.

Makes 12 servings.

2 lbs. ground beef
1 onion, chopped
2 10-3/4 oz. cans tomato soup
28-oz. can green beans, drained
salt and pepper to taste
1 c. shredded Cheddar cheese

Brown beef and onion together in a skillet; drain. Mix soup and beans in a lightly greased 13"x9" baking pan. Stir in beef mixture, salt and pepper; set aside. Spread Potato Topping evenly over mixture in pan; sprinkle with cheese. Bake, uncovered, at 350 degrees for about 30 minutes.

Potato Topping:
3 c. milk
3 c. water
1/4 c. margarine
1 t. salt
4 c. instant mashed potato flakes

Bring all ingredients except potato flakes to a boil. Stir in potato flakes; mix well. Cover and let stand for 5 minutes. If potatoes are too thick to spread, add milk or water to desired consistency.

Stephanie Moon, Nampa, ID

Ham & Pineapple Kabobs

Soak wooden kabob skewers in water at least 20 minutes before using...they won't burn or stick.

Makes 5 to 6 servings.

2 lbs. smoked ham, cut into 1-inch cubes
2 8-oz. cans pineapple chunks, drained and juice reserved
8 to 10 skewers, soaked in water
1/4 c. soy sauce
1/4 c. brown sugar, packed
1/4 t. ground ginger

Thread ham cubes and pineapple chunks on skewers; place in an ungreased 2-quart casserole dish. Combine reserved juice and remaining ingredients; pour over kabobs, turning to coat. Cover and refrigerate for 2 hours, turning occasionally. Grill over medium-hot coals, turning twice and brushing with marinade until hot and golden, about 10 minutes.

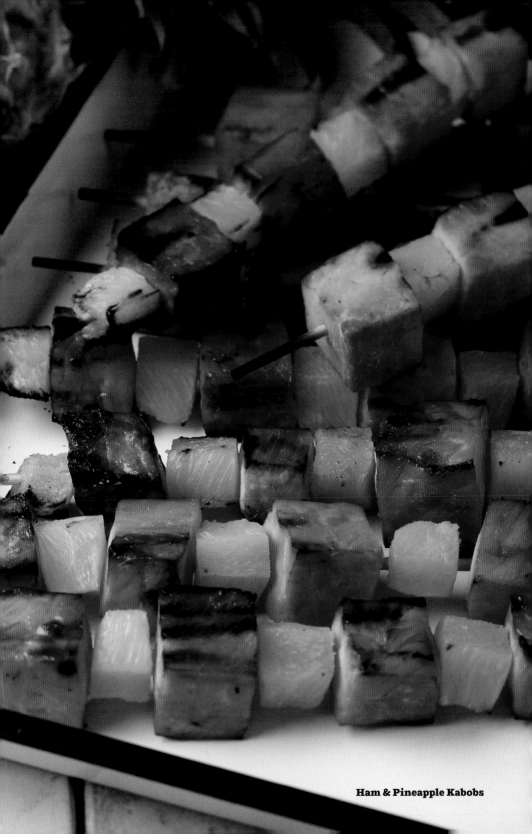

Ham & Pineapple Kabobs

Cara Lorenz, Olathe, CO

Creamed Ham on Cornbread

My family really enjoys the different flavors as a change of pace from meat & potato main dishes.

Makes 6 servings.

8-1/2 oz. pkg. corn muffin mix
1-1/2 c. plus 1/3 c. milk, divided
1 egg, beaten
2 T. butter
2 T. all-purpose flour
1/4 t. salt
3/4 c. shredded Cheddar cheese
1-1/2 c. cooked ham, cubed

Combine muffin mix, 1/3 cup milk and egg; mix well and pour into a greased 8"x8" baking pan. Bake at 400 degrees for 18 to 20 minutes. In a saucepan, melt butter over low heat. Stir in flour and salt. Slowly add remaining milk, whisking until smooth. Bring to a boil; boil and stir for 2 minutes. Stir in cheese and ham; heat through. Cut cornbread into squares; top with creamed ham.

Jennifer Niemi, Nova Scotia, Canada

Rosemary Peppers & Fusilli

This colorful, flavorful meatless meal is ready to serve in a jiffy. If you can't find fusilli pasta, try sea shells, rotini or even wagon wheels.

Makes 4 servings.

2 to 4 T. olive oil
2 red onions, thinly sliced and
    separated into rings
3 red, orange and/or yellow peppers,
    very thinly sliced
5 to 6 cloves garlic, very thinly sliced
3 T. dried rosemary
salt and pepper to taste
12-oz. pkg. fusilli pasta, cooked
Garnish: shredded mozzarella
    cheese

Add oil to a large skillet over medium heat. Add onions to skillet; cover and cook over medium heat for 10 minutes. Stir in remaining ingredients except pasta and cheese; reduce heat. Cook, covered, stirring occasionally, for an additional 20 minutes. Serve vegetable mixture over pasta, topped with cheese.

Rosemary Peppers & Fusilli

Renee Strickland, Gainesville, GA

Renee's Skillet Ham & Tomatoes

I came up with this recipe myself and my family loves it...I'm sure yours will love it also! It's a delicious quick-fix meal, wonderful served with a tossed salad and hot rolls.

Serves 8.

1 T. cornstarch
1 to 2 T. cold water
2 T. margarine
1 onion, chopped
2 c. cooked ham, chopped
2 14-1/2 oz. cans diced tomatoes
3 c. cooked rice
1 to 2 T. soy sauce
salt and pepper to taste

Mix cornstarch and water; set aside. Melt margarine in a skillet over medium heat. Add onion and ham; sauté until onion is opaque. Add tomatoes with juice to skillet. Bring to a boil; stir in cornstarch mixture and cook until thickened. Turn down to low heat and add remaining ingredients. Cook and stir until heated through.

Kris Coburn, Dansville, NY

Buffalo Chicken Pizza

Hot pepper sauce is available in several flavors and heat levels... choose one that's to your liking!

Serves 4 to 6.

12-inch Italian pizza crust
1/4 c. butter, melted
1/4 c. hot pepper sauce
2 c. cooked chicken, diced
1/2 c. celery, chopped
4-oz. pkg. crumbled blue cheese

Place crust on a lightly greased 12" pizza pan; set aside. Combine butter and pepper sauce; mix well. Add chicken and celery, tossing to coat. Spread chicken mixture evenly over crust. Sprinkle with cheese. Bake at 450 degrees for 10 to 12 minutes, or until heated through and crust is crisp.

Buffalo Chicken Pizza

Easy Slow-Cooker Steak, Page 180

CHAPTER FOUR

Slow-Cooker, Make-Ahead & Freezer-Friendly

Mexican Dump Chicken, Page 164

Cheesy Chicken, Page 174

Michelle Collins, San Diego, CA

Collins' Best Lentil Soup

Thanks to the hearty ingredients this soup offers, appetites are sure to be well satisfied.

Makes about 10 cups.

1 c. dried lentils, rinsed
14-oz. pkg. turkey Kielbasa, sliced
   1/2-inch thick
6 c. beef broth
1 c. onion, chopped
1 c. celery, chopped
1 c. carrots, peeled and chopped
1 c. redskin potato, diced
2 T. fresh flat-leaf parsley, chopped
1/2 t. pepper
1/8 t. ground nutmeg

Combine all ingredients in a 3-quart slow cooker. Cover and cook on high setting for one hour. Reduce heat to low setting and cook 3 hours. Stir before serving.

Susie Rogers, Puyallup, WA

Avocado Dip

Add a bit of diced red onion or pimento for extra flavor and color!

Makes about 2 cups.

2 avocados, pitted, peeled and
   chopped
8-oz. pkg. cream cheese, softened
1/4 c. mayonnaise
1/2 to 1 t. garlic salt

Blend all ingredients together; cover and chill until serving.

★ DID YOU KNOW? ★ **A covered slow cooker cooks with little or no evaporation...all the delicious cooking juices combine to create a scrumptious gravy. Just add the amount of liquid that the recipe calls for.**

Collins' Best Lentil Soup

Joanne Curran, Arlington, MA

Slow-Cooker Country Chicken & Dumplings

Using a slow cooker and a package of refrigerated biscuits, this recipe is a lifesaver on busy weeknights.

Serves 6.

4 boneless, skinless chicken breasts
2 10-3/4 oz. cans cream of chicken
   soup
2 T. butter, sliced
1 onion, finely diced
2 7-1/2 oz. tubes refrigerated
   biscuits, torn

Add chicken, soup, butter and onion to a 4-quart slow cooker; add enough water to cover chicken. Cover and cook on high setting for 4 hours. Add biscuits to slow cooker; gently push biscuits into cooking liquid. Cover and continue cooking for about 1-1/2 hours, until biscuits are done in the center.

Helen Burns, Raleigh, NC

Snowstorm Beef Stew

This recipe's ingredient list may seem a little unusual! I came up with it during a winter storm, using what we had in the pantry and freezer. We've enjoyed this stew ever since.

Makes 4 to 6 servings.

2 lbs. stew beef cubes
18-1/2 oz. can French onion soup
16-oz. container sour cream onion
   dip
2 13-1/4 oz. cans mixed vegetables,
   drained
1 c. elbow macaroni, uncooked

Place beef in a slow cooker; pour soup over top. Cover and cook on high setting for 3 hours. Stir in dip; cover and cook for an additional 2 hours, stirring occasionally. Add vegetables and uncooked macaroni. Cover and cook on high setting for one additional hour, or until macaroni is tender.

★ FREEZE IT ★ A large-size slow cooker tends dinner for you all day long. It can easily handle a double batch of a favorite recipe too. Serve half tonight...cool the other half and freeze for a future meal.

Slow-Cooker Country Chicken & Dumplings

Erin McRae, Beaverton, OR

Slow-Cooker Beefy Taco Soup

Top each bowl of this hearty soup with sour cream and a sprinkling of shredded cheese.

Serves 4 to 6.

1 lb. ground beef
1-1/4 oz. pkg. taco seasoning mix
15-oz. can stewed tomatoes
8-oz. can tomato sauce
15-oz. can kidney beans, drained and rinsed

Brown beef in a skillet over medium heat. Drain; stir in taco seasoning. Add tomatoes with juice, tomato sauce and beans; transfer to a 3-quart slow cooker. Cover and cook on low setting for 6 to 8 hours, stirring occasionally.

Tami Hoffman, Litchfield, NH

Slow-Cooker Creamy Apricot Chicken

Serve with creamy mashed potatoes and your favorite veggie. Then pour on spoonfuls of the creamy apricot sauce.

Serves 4 to 6.

1 to 2 lbs. boneless, skinless chicken breasts
12-oz. jar apricot preserves
8-oz. bottle Russian salad dressing

Arrange chicken in a 4-quart slow cooker; set aside. Combine preserves and salad dressing; spoon over chicken. Cover and cook on high setting for one hour. Reduce heat to low and cook for 3 hours, or until chicken juices run clear.

★ DOUBLE DUTY ★ Some foods taste even better the second day. Slow-cook overnight, then in the morning cool and spoon into a food storage container to refrigerate. At dinnertime, reheat on the stovetop until piping hot... mmm!

Slow-Cooker Creamy Apricot Chicken

Kimberly Lyons, Commerce, TX

Chicken & Wild Rice

Mmm...great with fresh-baked bread and a green salad. Freezes beautifully!

Serves 6 to 8.

2 6.2-oz. pkgs. quick-cooking
　long-grain and wild rice mix
　with seasoning packets
4 boneless, skinless chicken breasts,
　cut into 1-inch cubes
10-3/4 oz. can cream of mushroom
　soup
1-1/3 c. frozen mixed vegetables,
　thawed
3 c. water

Gently stir together all ingredients. Spread into an ungreased 13"x9" baking pan. Bake, uncovered, at 350 degrees for about 45 minutes, stirring occasionally, until juices run clear when chicken is pierced with a fork.

Lora Burek, Irwin, PA

Pennsylvania Stuffed Peppers

The perfect comfort food...they taste even better the next day! Mashed potatoes are heavenly topped with some of the sauce from the peppers.

Serves 6.

1-1/2 lbs. ground beef
1 egg, beaten
1 c. orzo pasta or instant rice,
　uncooked
garlic salt and pepper to taste
6 green, yellow or red peppers, tops
　removed
2 10-3/4 oz. cans tomato soup
2-1/2 c. water

Mix beef, egg, uncooked orzo or rice and seasonings in a bowl. Stuff peppers lightly with mixture. If any extra beef mixture remains, form into small meatballs. In a slow cooker, blend together soup and water. Arrange stuffed peppers in slow cooker; replace tops on peppers for a nice touch. Place meatballs around peppers. Lightly spoon some of soup mixture onto tops of peppers. Cover and cook on low setting for 8 to 10 hours.

★ TIME-SAVING SHORTCUT ★ Take advantage of your slow cooker on weekends too. Put dinner in the crock Saturday morning, then take the kids on a hike, shop or relax around the house. Dinner is ready when you are!

Chicken & Wild Rice

Julie Pak, Henryetta, OK

Smoky Hobo Dinner

Away from home all day? This slow-cooker creation will have dinner waiting for you!

Serves 6.

5 potatoes, peeled and quartered
1 head cabbage, coarsely chopped
16-oz. pkg. baby carrots
1 onion, thickly sliced
salt and pepper to taste
14-oz. pkg. smoked pork sausage, sliced into 2-inch pieces
1/2 c. water

Spray a slow cooker with non-stick vegetable spray. Layer vegetables in slow cooker, sprinkling each layer with salt and pepper. Place sausage on top. Pour water down one side of slow cooker. Cover and cook on low setting for 6 to 8 hours.

Angie Whitmore, Farmington, UT

Angie's Pasta & Sauce

This homemade sauce is so simple to prepare, especially the night before. You'll love the sauce with freshly shredded Parmesan on top.

Serves 4 to 6.

8-oz. pkg. angel hair pasta, uncooked
6 to 8 roma tomatoes, halved and diced
1 to 2 cloves garlic, minced
1/2 c. butter, melted
1 T. dried basil
Garnish: shredded Parmesan cheese

Cook pasta according to package directions; drain. Meanwhile, combine tomatoes and garlic in a saucepan. Simmer over medium heat for 15 minutes; set aside. Blend together butter and basil; add to cooked pasta and toss to coat. Stir tomato mixture into pasta; garnish as desired.

★ DID YOU KNOW? ★ Soft veggies like peas and spinach don't need to cook all day. Stir them into the crock in the last 30 minutes...they'll keep their fresh color and firm texture.

Angie's Pasta & Sauce

Lisa Ludwig, Fort Wayne, IN

Cantonese Dinner

This recipe is a family favorite. Whether served over rice or chow mein noodles, it's full of flavor!

Serves 4.

1-1/2 to 2 lbs. boneless beef round steak, cut into strips
1 T. oil
1 onion, chopped
1 green pepper, chopped
3 4-oz. cans sliced mushrooms, drained
8-oz. can tomato sauce
3 T. brown sugar, packed
1-1/2 T. vinegar
2 t. Worcestershire sauce
1-1/2 t. salt

In a skillet over medium heat, brown beef strips in oil; drain. Combine beef, onion, green pepper and mushrooms in a 4-quart slow cooker. Combine remaining ingredients in a small bowl and mix well; pour over beef and vegetables. Cover and cook on low setting for 6 to 8 hours, or on high setting for 3 hours.

Marcia Bills, Orleans, NE

Hearty Lasagna Soup

My daughters request this soup whenever they are coming home from college for weekends or holidays...in fact, our family calls it Coming Home Soup! It's so warm and delicious, we all love it.

Makes 6 servings.

1 lb. ground beef, browned and drained
6.4-oz. pkg. ground beef lasagna dinner, divided
6 c. water
1 c. corn
15-oz. can Italian-style stewed tomatoes

Place beef in a slow cooker. Add lasagna sauce mix, water, corn and undrained tomatoes; stir well. Cover and cook on low setting for 4 to 6 hours. Mix in lasagna noodles and cook an additional 20 minutes, until noodles are tender.

Cantonese Dinner

SLOW COOKER, MAKE-AHEAD & FREEZER-FRIENDLY

Ashley Whitehead, Sidney, TX

Easy Round Steak

Do you like lots of gravy? Use two packages of soup mix and two cans of soup.

Serves 5.

2 to 2-1/2 lbs. beef round steak, cut
   into serving-size pieces
10-3/4 oz. can cream of mushroom
   soup
1/4 c. water
1-1/2 oz. pkg. onion soup mix

Place beef in a 4-quart slow cooker. Add soup mix, water and soup. Cover and cook on low setting for 6 to 8 hours.

Trisha Brady, Richmond, VA

Italian Sausage & Penne

Pop some garlic bread in the oven... dinner is ready!

Serves 4.

3/4 lb. hot Italian pork sausage links,
   cut into bite-size pieces
1 red pepper, chopped
1/2 onion, chopped
26-oz. jar spaghetti sauce
8-oz. pkg. penne pasta, cooked

Stir together all ingredients except pasta in a 3-quart slow cooker. Cover and cook on low setting for 7 to 8 hours. At serving time, stir in cooked pasta.

★ TIME-SAVING SHORTCUT ★
After you unpack groceries, take just a little time to prep ingredients and place them in plastic zipping bags...wash and chop fruits and vegetables, place meats in marinades and so forth.

Italian Sausage & Penne

Alice Ardaugh, Joliet, IL

Zesty Italian Chicken

Not your usual chicken dinner!

Serves 4.

4 boneless, skinless chicken breasts
1/2 c. Italian salad dressing, divided
1/2 c. grated Parmesan cheese,
   divided
1 t. Italian seasoning, divided
4 potatoes, quartered

Arrange chicken in a 4-quart slow cooker; sprinkle with half each of salad dressing, Parmesan cheese and Italian seasoning. Add potatoes; top with remaining dressing, cheese and seasoning. Cover and cook on low setting for 8 hours, or on high setting for 4 hours.

Melinda Hokoth, Rockford, IL

Pulled Beef Sandwiches

Serve this tender beef spooned onto toasted hoagie rolls, topped with slices of mozzarella cheese...delicious!

Makes 4 to 6 servings.

2-lb. beef chuck roast
garlic powder, salt and pepper
   to taste
1/2 t. meat tenderizer
1 c. beef broth
1-1/4 c. water
1.35-oz. pkg. onion soup mix

Sprinkle roast with seasonings and tenderizer; place in a slow cooker. Pour in broth and water. Cover and cook on low setting for 8 to 10 hours. When roast is very tender, shred with 2 forks. Stir in soup mix and continue cooking for 30 minutes.

★ TIME-SAVING SHORTCUT ★ Oven roasting bags speed up the baking time for ham, pot roast and turkey. Clean-up is a breeze too... just toss away the mess.

Zesty Italian Chicken

Connie Gabbard, Athens, OH

Poppy Seed Chicken

Don't be tempted to sprinkle on the cracker-crumb mixture while the chicken is in the slow cooker... condensation will make the topping soggy.

Serves 6.

6 boneless, skinless chicken breasts
2 10-3/4 oz. cans cream of chicken
   soup
1 c. milk
1 T. poppy seed
36 round buttery crackers, crushed
1/4 c. butter, melted

Place chicken in a lightly greased 5-quart slow cooker. Whisk together soup, milk and poppy seed in a bowl; spoon over chicken. Cover and cook on high setting for one hour. Reduce heat to low setting; cover and cook for 3 hours. Combine cracker crumbs and butter in a bowl, stirring until crumbs are moistened. Sprinkle over chicken just before serving.

Jessica Shrout, Flintstone, MD

Slow-Cooker Scalloped Potatoes

A rich and cheesy adaptation of a favorite baked recipe. It's wonderful for potlucks and get-togethers. Sometimes I'll add a few unpeeled, sliced redskin potatoes for a bit of color.

Makes 8 to 10 servings.

4 lbs. potatoes, peeled, sliced and
   divided
2 T. butter, sliced
1 onion, diced and divided
16-oz. pkg. thick-cut bacon, diced
   and divided
3 c. shredded Cheddar cheese,
   divided
8-oz. pkg. cream cheese, cubed and
   divided
2 10-3/4 oz. cans cream of chicken
   soup
dried parsley, salt and pepper to
   taste

Arrange half of the potato slices in a large slow cooker; dot with butter. Top with half each of the onion, uncooked bacon and cheeses; repeat layers. Top with soup and seasonings. Cover and cook on low setting for 8 to 10 hours, until bubbly and potatoes are tender.

Slow-Cooker Scalloped Potatoes

Irene Robinson, Cincinnati, OH

Zesty Mustard Sauce

Make this ahead of time and keep it in the fridge. Delicious on hot steamed broccoli, asparagus spears or green beans.

Makes about 2 cups.

3/4 c. mayonnaise
3 T. lemon juice
1-1/2 T. Dijon mustard
1/2 c. heavy cream

In a bowl, mix together mayonnaise, lemon juice and mustard; set aside. In a separate bowl, with an electric mixer on high speed, beat cream until soft peaks form. Fold whipped cream into mayonnaise mixture. Keep refrigerated.

Vickie, Gooseberry Patch

Sour Cream Chicken

It doesn't get any easier than this...and soo delicious!

Makes 4 servings.

4 boneless, skinless chicken breasts
16-oz. container sour cream
5-1/2 oz. pkg. baked chicken coating
   mix
mashed potatoes

Arrange chicken in a slow cooker. Mix together sour cream and coating mix; spoon over chicken. Cover and cook on low setting for 4 to 5 hours. Serve chicken over mashed potatoes.

★ FREEZE IT ★ Frozen veggies are oh-so handy for cooking up tasty slow-cooker dishes. Thaw them overnight in the fridge or rinse with cool water before adding... they won't slow down the heating process.

Sour Cream Chicken

Tara Horton, Delaware, OH

Zesty Chicken Barbecue

This recipe is a staple at our house... we all love it! There are so many tasty varieties of bottled barbecue sauce on the market that I can easily change it up by using a different flavor.

Serves 6.

6 boneless, skinless chicken breasts
1-1/2 c. barbecue sauce
1/2 c. zesty Italian salad dressing
1/4 c. brown sugar, packed
2 T. Worcestershire sauce

Arrange chicken breasts in a slow cooker. Blend together remaining ingredients and pour over chicken. Cover and cook on low setting for 6 to 8 hours.

Dana Andrews, Marysville, TN

Company Chicken & Stuffing

Sometimes I use Pepper Jack cheese instead of Swiss. It's delicious!

Serves 4.

4 boneless, skinless chicken breasts
4 slices Swiss cheese
6-oz. pkg. chicken-flavored stuffing mix
2 10-3/4 oz. cans cream of chicken soup
1/2 c. chicken broth

Arrange chicken in a slow cooker; top each piece with a slice of cheese. Mix together stuffing mix, broth and soup; spoon into slow cooker. Cover and cook on low setting for 6 to 8 hours.

★ TIME-SAVING SHORTCUT ★ Root vegetables like carrots and potatoes take longer to cook than meat. Cube or slice them evenly and place in the bottom of the slow cooker before adding the meat.

Company Chicken & Stuffing

Angela Lively, Baxter, TN

Country Corn Pudding

With four kinds of corn, this new twist on an old favorite is sure to be scrumptious!

Makes 8 servings.

16-oz. pkg. frozen corn
2 11-oz. cans sweet corn & diced peppers
14-3/4 oz. can creamed corn
6-1/2 oz. pkg. corn muffin mix
3/4 c. water
1/4 c. butter, melted
1 t. salt

Mix all ingredients well; pour into a slow cooker. Cover and cook on low setting for 5 to 6 hours, stirring after 3 hours.

Ramona Storm, Gardner, IL

Easy Chicken & Noodles

This smells so good and warms you up on a cold day. Leftover cooked chicken works great. Add some warm, crusty bread and a citrus salad...dinner is served!

Makes 8 servings.

16-oz. pkg. frozen egg noodles, uncooked
2 14-1/2 oz. cans chicken broth
2 10-3/4 oz. cans cream of chicken soup
1/2 c. onion, finely chopped
1/2 c. carrot, peeled and diced
1/2 c. celery, diced
salt and pepper to taste
2 c. boneless, skinless chicken breasts, cooked and cubed

Thaw egg noodles (or run package under warm water) just enough to break apart; set aside. Spray a slow cooker with non-stick vegetable spray. Add remaining ingredients except chicken; blend well. Stir in noodles and chicken. Cover and cook on low setting for 7 to 8 hours, until hot and bubbly.

Easy Chicken & Noodles

Staci Allen, Sheboygan, WI

Maple Whiskey Ribs

We are always given fresh maple syrup around the holidays. Our family is not into breakfast, so we enjoy using the syrup in different meat dishes. Enjoy these ribs with buttered noodles or warm bread.

Makes 4 servings.

1/2 c. pure maple syrup
1/4 c. whiskey or fruit juice
2 T. Dijon mustard
2 lbs. pork spareribs, cut into
    serving-size sections
1 large purple onion, sliced

In a small bowl, whisk together syrup, whiskey or juice and mustard. Brush mixture over spareribs. Place ribs in a slow cooker; top with onion slices. Cover and cook on low setting for 6 to 8 hours, until ribs are very tender.

Amy Woods, Collinsville, TX

Kickin' Pork Chops

I love these quick & easy chops! My son Stephen puts them on when he gets home from high school. I simply add sides like boiled new potatoes and steamed Brussels sprouts for a healthy weeknight meal we enjoy.

Makes 4 to 6 servings.

4 to 6 thick-cut boneless pork chops
10-3/4 oz. can cream of chicken soup
1-oz. pkg. ranch salad dressing mix
1 T. Creole seasoning

Spray a slow cooker with non-stick cooking spray. Lay pork chops in slow cooker and set aside. Mix remaining ingredients in a bowl; spoon over pork chops. Cover and cook on low setting for 4 to 5 hours, until pork chops are tender.

★ DOUBLE DUTY ★ Savory slow-cooker recipes fit everyone's schedule, and the wonderful aroma of home-cooked food greets you at the door!

Kickin' Pork Chops

Mindy Humphrey, Evansville, IN

Mexican Dump Chicken

Toss this simple recipe into the slow cooker first thing in the morning. Hardly any prep is required! Leftovers freeze well too.

Makes 8 servings.

3 boneless, skinless chicken breasts
15-oz. can corn, drained
15-oz. can black beans, drained and
    rinsed
8-oz. jar salsa
1 onion, coarsely chopped
8-oz. pkg. cream cheese, cubed
taco shells or tortilla chips

Place chicken breasts in a slow cooker. Top with corn, beans, salsa and onion. Cover and cook on low setting for 6 to 8 hours, until chicken is tender. About 30 minutes before serving, shred chicken in slow cooker. Add the cream cheese; stir to combine. Cover and cook on low setting for 30 minutes, or until cream cheese has melted. Serve chicken mixture with taco shells or tortilla chips.

Barbara Hightower, Broomfield, CO

Healthy Crock Burritos

My daughter Gigi gave me this easy recipe for chicken burritos after she served them to us for family dinner at her house. Great for filling up the slow cooker and coming home to a hot meal...they're low-calorie and really delicious!

Makes 4 to 6 servings.

4 boneless, skinless chicken breasts
15-oz. can black beans, drained and
    rinsed
7-oz. can red enchilada sauce
7-oz. can green enchilada sauce
burrito-size flour tortillas
Garnish: chopped onions,
    shredded lettuce, sour cream,
    shredded Cheddar cheese

Arrange chicken breasts in a slow cooker. Layer beans and sauces over chicken. Cover and cook on low setting for 6 to 8 hours. Remove chicken to a plate; shred with a fork. Return chicken to slow cooker and stir to mix. To serve, spoon chicken mixture into tortillas; add desired toppings and roll up.

Mexican Dump Chicken

Kiersten Adams, Marion, OH

Pineapple Chicken

This recipe couldn't be easier, and it smells wonderful when I walk in the door after work!

Serves 4 to 6.

3 to 4 lbs. boneless, skinless chicken
16-oz. bottle Catalina salad dressing
20-oz. can pineapple chunks, drained
   and 1/4 cup juice reserved

Place chicken in slow cooker. Add salad dressing, pineapple and reserved juice. Cover and cook on low setting for 8 to 9 hours, or on high setting for 6 hours.

Brenna Carey, Shickshinny, PA

Slow-Cooker Sage Stuffing

I use this recipe every Thanksgiving because it's so delicious...it frees up space in the oven too.

Makes 8 to 10 servings.

14 c. bread cubes
3 c. celery, chopped
1-1/2 c. onion, chopped
1-1/2 t. to 1 T. dried sage
1 t. salt
1/2 t. pepper
1-1/4 c. butter, melted

In a very large bowl, combine all ingredients except butter; mix well. Add butter and toss. Spoon into a lightly greased slow cooker. Cover and cook on low setting 4 to 5 hours.

★ TIME-SAVING SHORTCUT ★ **Adapt family favorites like chili or beef stew to the slow cooker. A dish that simmers for 2 hours on the stovetop can generally cook all day on the low setting without overcooking.**

Pineapple Chicken

Mary Alice Veal, Mars Hill, NC

Slow-Cooked Mac & Cheese

This tastes just like the old-fashioned macaroni & cheese that Grandma used to make. It is delicious and oh-so easy!

Makes 6 to 8 servings.

8-oz. pkg. elbow macaroni, cooked
2 eggs, beaten
12-oz. can evaporated milk
1-1/2 c. milk
3 c. shredded sharp Cheddar cheese
1/2 c. margarine, melted
1 t. salt
pepper to taste

Mix all ingredients together and pour into a lightly greased slow cooker. Cover and cook on low setting for 3 to 4 hours.

Howard Cooper, Palo Alto, CA

Montana Wild Rice Beef Stew

I grew up in Montana, and this reminds me of the soup my mom made on those very cold winter nights.

Serves 6.

4 c. sliced mushrooms
3 carrots, peeled and sliced 1/2-inch thick
6-oz. pkg. long-grain and wild rice
1 lb. beef sirloin, cubed
5 c. beef broth

Combine mushrooms, carrots and rice mix with seasoning packet in a slow cooker. Top with beef; pour broth over top. Cover and cook on low setting for 8 to 10 hours.

★ TIME-SAVING SHORTCUT ★ Slice and dice meats and veggies ahead of time and refrigerate in separate plastic zipping bags. In the morning, toss everything into the slow cooker and you're on your way.

Montana Wild Rice Beef Stew

Jessica Sanchez, Houston, TX

Zippy Shredded Pork

Sometimes I top these with a little bit of coleslaw. So good!

Makes 6 servings.

2 to 3-lb. boneless pork loin roast
salt and pepper to taste
16-oz. jar salsa
Optional: hot pepper sauce, chopped
   green chiles
6 hard rolls, split

Place roast in a slow cooker; sprinkle with salt and pepper. Pour salsa over roast; add hot sauce or chiles for extra heat, if desired. Cover and cook on low setting for 8 to 10 hours, until meat shreds easily. Stir meat to shred completely and serve on rolls.

Margaret Hart, Lexington, KY

Slow-Cooker Chicken Tacolados

My family likes these topped with shredded cheese and diced green onions.

Serves 6 to 8.

5 boneless, skinless chicken thighs
2 boneless, skinless chicken breasts
10-oz. can green enchilada sauce
10-3/4 oz. can cream of chicken soup
12 to 15 10-inch flour tortillas,
   warmed
Garnish: salsa

Arrange chicken pieces in a slow cooker; set aside. Combine sauce and soup in a bowl; blend well and pour over chicken. Cover and cook on low setting for 8 hours, or on high setting for 4 hours. When chicken is tender, shred with 2 forks. Serve on warmed tortillas; garnish as desired.

★ FREEZE IT ★ **It's easy to save leftover fresh herbs. Spoon chopped herbs into an ice cube tray, one tablespoon per cube. Cover with water and freeze. Frozen cubes can be dropped right into hot stew or soup.**

Zippy Shredded Pork

Vickie Zettler, Springfield, OH

My Famous Shredded Chicken

I grew up in a family where my mother and grandmother made everything from scratch. Later, as a single mother raising two sons with "hollow legs," I sometimes had to invent recipes that produced not only quality but quantity. I've been making this for years, and the other day one of my sons called to ask me for the recipe. He's 43 years old now...I was so happy!

Makes 8 to 10 servings.

40-oz. pkg. frozen boneless, skinless
   chicken tenderloins
10-3/4 oz. can cream of mushroom
   soup
10-3/4 oz. can cream of chicken soup
10-3/4 oz. can cream of celery soup
salt and pepper to taste
8 to 10 sandwich buns, or cooked rice
   or noodles

Place chicken in a slow cooker, separating pieces. Top with soups; season with salt and pepper. Cover and cook on low setting for 8 to 10 hours, until chicken is very tender. Uncover; shred chicken with 2 forks and stir into soup mixture. Continue cooking, uncovered, for about 30 minutes, until gravy is thick. Serve chicken mixture spooned onto buns or ladled over rice or noodles.

Judy Williams, Oil Springs, KY

Judy's Easy Meatloaf

This slow-cooker meatloaf is great for busy cooks! It's easy to adjust the seasonings to your family's preference. Try using hot pork sausage if you enjoy spicy flavors.

Serves 8 to 10.

2 to 3 lbs. ground beef
1 lb. ground pork sausage
1-1/2 c. long-cooking oats, uncooked
2 eggs, beaten
3/4 c. evaporated milk
1 onion, chopped
6 T. sugar
2 T. chili powder
1 t. salt
1/2 t. pepper
14-1/2 oz. can diced tomatoes

Combine all ingredients except tomatoes and mix well. Shape into a loaf; place in an oval slow cooker. Cover with undrained tomatoes. Cover and cook on low setting for 6 to 8 hours, or 2 to 4 hours on high setting.

★ **TIME-SAVING SHORTCUT** ★
It's fine to fill a slow cooker with chilled ingredients, then set the timer to start one to 2 hours later. If yours doesn't have a timer, pick up an automatic timer at the hardware store and plug the crock right into it.

My Famous Shredded Chicken

Jenifer Rutland, Hiawatha, KS

Cheesy Chicken

Slow-cooker meals are always the easiest for me. This one is a hit with the kids! The chicken is very tender and juicy. I serve it with mashed potatoes and use the cheesy sauce as a gravy.

Makes 6 to 8 servings.

6 to 8 boneless, skinless chicken
   breasts
1/2 c. butter, melted
10-3/4 oz. can cream of chicken soup
8-oz. container sour cream
1 onion, chopped
1 c. shredded Colby Jack cheese
salt and pepper to taste
8-oz. pkg. pasteurized process cheese,
   cubed

Place chicken in a slow cooker; drizzle with butter and set aside. In a bowl, combine soup, sour cream, onion, shredded cheese, salt and pepper. Mix well and pour over chicken. Add just enough water to cover ingredients. Add cheese cubes on top. Cover and cook on low setting for 6 to 8 hours.

Ethel Carpenter, Fargo, ND

Slow-Cooker Ham

We love this with corn pudding served on the side!

Serves 8 to 10.

6 to 8-lb. picnic ham, trimmed
64-oz. bottle apple juice
1 c. brown sugar, packed
3 to 4 T. apple jelly
2 T. maple syrup

Trim skin and excess fat from ham. Place onto a cutting board. With a sharp knife, score ham in a diamond pattern, making cuts about one to 1-1/2 inches apart. Place ham into slow cooker flat-side down. Pour in enough apple juice to cover. Cover and cook on low setting for 6 hours. Transfer to a lightly greased baking sheet; set aside. Mix brown sugar, apple jelly and maple syrup together in a bowl; spread onto ham. Bake at 375 degrees for 30 to 40 minutes, until topping is bubbling and glazed.

Cheesy Chicken

Joyceann Dreibelbis, Wooster, OH

Sloppy Jane Sandwiches

This simple slow-cooker recipe is easily doubled for a tailgating party with friends.

Serves 6 to 8.

16-oz. pkg. hot dogs, sliced 3/4-inch
   thick
28-oz. can baked beans
1/3 c. chili sauce
1 t. dried, minced onion
1 t. mustard
6 to 8 hot dog buns, split and toasted

In a slow cooker, stir together all ingredients except buns. Cover and cook on low setting for 2 to 3 hours. To serve, spoon into buns.

Jo Ann, Gooseberry Patch

Oh-So-Easy Lasagna

This recipe is so easy to customize with what you have on hand. Really, any flavor pasta sauce will work, and feel free to try it with ground turkey or pork if you like.

Serves 8.

1 to 2 lbs. ground beef, browned and
   drained
26-oz. jar Parmesan & Romano pasta
   sauce
8-oz. pkg. bowtie pasta, cooked
12-oz. container cottage cheese
16-oz. pkg. shredded mozzarella
   cheese

Mix together ground beef and pasta sauce. In a slow cooker, layer half each of ground beef mixture, pasta, cottage cheese and shredded cheese. Repeat with remaining ingredients. Cover and cook on low setting for 6 to 8 hours, or on high setting for 3 to 4 hours.

★ **DID YOU KNOW?** ★ **No peeking!** Lifting the lid of your slow cooker releases heat and can lengthen the cooking time.

Oh-So-Easy Lasagna

Tina Wright, Atlanta, GA

One-Dish Tuna & Noodles

This is one of those simple dishes we all remember from childhood. Make this on a Sunday afternoon and freeze it for later in the week!

Serves 4 to 6.

1 c. egg noodles, uncooked
10-3/4 oz. can cream of mushroom soup
2/3 c. water
2 t. chopped pimentos
1 c. American cheese, chopped
7-oz. can tuna, drained

Cook noodles according to package directions; drain. Meanwhile, combine soup and water in a saucepan over medium heat. Cook until smooth, stirring frequently. Fold in pimentos and cheese; stir until cheese melts. Remove from heat and set aside. Combine tuna and noodles in a bowl and mix well; spoon into a lightly greased shallow 2-quart casserole dish. Pour cheese mixture on top; stir gently to mix. Bake, uncovered, at 375 degrees for 30 minutes, until hot and bubbly.

Jill Burton, Gooseberry Patch

Herb-Seasoned Spinach Puffs

Serve with a spicy mustard sauce for dipping.

Serves 8 to 10.

2 10-oz. pkgs. frozen chopped spinach, thawed
2 c. herb-flavored stuffing mix
1 c. grated Parmesan cheese
6 eggs, lightly beaten
1/3 c. butter, softened

Drain and squeeze spinach to remove all liquid. Combine spinach with remaining ingredients. Mix well and form into 2-inch balls; place on a lightly greased baking sheet. Cover with aluminum foil and refrigerate overnight. Bake at 350 degrees for 15 minutes, or until heated through; remove from baking sheet and cool on paper towels.

Herb-Seasoned Spinach Puffs

Sandy Springs, Indianapolis, IN

Easy Slow-Cooker Steak

I've been making this dish for years and my family never gets tired of it!

Makes 5 servings.

2 to 2-1/2 lb. beef round steak, cut
    into bite-size pieces
1-1/2 oz. pkg. onion soup mix
1/4 c. water
10-3/4 oz. can cream of mushroom
    soup

Place beef in a slow cooker. Add soup mix, water and soup. Cover and cook on low setting for 6 to 8 hours.

Liz Plotnick-Snay, Gooseberry Patch

Icebox Slaw

Make this slaw when your garden is bursting with crisp cabbage...savor it for months to come.

Serves 6 to 8.

1 head cabbage, shredded
1 t. salt
2 carrots, peeled and grated
1 c. cider vinegar
1 c. sugar
1/4 c. fresh parsley, chopped
1/4 c. water

Combine cabbage and salt in a large saucepan; cover and let stand one hour. Drain liquid from pan and add carrots. Combine remaining ingredients in a bowl; whisk until well blended. Pour vinegar mixture over cabbage mixture in pan and toss to mix; place over medium heat and bring to a boil. Cook for one minute; remove from heat and cool. Place slaw in airtight containers or plastic zipping bags and freeze up to 3 months; thaw several hours before serving.

★ TIME-SAVING SHORTCUT ★
Check the liquid in the slow cooker about 30 minutes before done cooking. If it seems too juicy, just remove the lid and turn the setting up to high...excess liquid will evaporate.

Easy Slow-Cooker Steak

Cherries & Cream Muffins, Page 192

CHAPTER FIVE

Breads, Muffins & Rolls

Italian Bread, Page 196

Sharon's Banana Muffins, Page 208

Cheri Henry, Newalla, OK

Strawberry Surprise Biscuits

Whole strawberries are hidden inside these biscuits, which are sweetened with a powdered sugar glaze.

Makes one dozen.

2 c. all-purpose flour
1 T. baking powder
1/2 t. salt
2 T. sugar
1/4 c. butter
3/4 c. plus 1 T. milk, divided
12 strawberries, hulled
2/3 c. powdered sugar
1/4 t. vanilla extract

Combine flour, baking powder, salt and sugar in a large bowl. Cut in butter with a pastry blender or 2 forks until mixture is crumbly. Add 3/4 cup milk, stirring just until moistened. Turn dough out onto a lightly floured surface; knead 4 to 5 times. Divide dough into 12 pieces. Pat pieces into 3-inch circles on a floured surface. Place a strawberry in the center of each circle. Bring dough edges up over strawberries; pinch ends to seal. Place biscuits on a lightly greased baking sheet. Bake at 425 degrees for 18 to 20 minutes, until golden. Stir together powdered sugar, remaining milk and vanilla for glaze. Cool biscuits and drizzle with glaze.

Denise Webb, Newington, GA

Amber's Cinnamon Bread

This recipe was always my daughter's favorite quick bread. Now as a mommy, she loves to make it for her kids.

Makes one loaf.

1 egg, beaten
1/4 c. oil
1-1/2 c. sugar, divided
2 c. all-purpose flour
1/2 t. salt
1 t. baking soda
1 c. buttermilk
1 T. cinnamon

In a large bowl, beat together egg, oil and one cup sugar; set aside. In a separate bowl, mix together flour, salt and baking soda. Add flour mixture to egg mixture alternately with buttermilk, stirring well. Combine cinnamon and remaining sugar in a cup. Spoon half of batter into a greased 9"x5" loaf pan; sprinkle with half of cinnamon-sugar. Repeat layers; swirl with a knife. Bake at 350 degrees for one hour. Cool for 10 minutes; turn out of pan.

Strawberry Surprise Biscuits

Jeanne Barringer, Edgewater, FL

Sour Cream Mini Biscuits

This recipe makes several dozen bite-size biscuits...ideal for filling gift baskets or taking to a potluck.

Makes 4 dozen.

1 c. butter, softened
1 c. sour cream
2 c. self-rising flour

Blend butter and sour cream together until fluffy; gradually mix in flour. Drop teaspoonfuls of dough into greased mini muffin cups. Bake at 450 degrees for 10 to 12 minutes.

Jo Ann, Gooseberry Patch

Parmesan-Garlic Biscuits

These upside-down biscuits are a hit with any Italian dish!

Serves 8.

3 T. butter, melted
1/4 t. celery seed
2 cloves garlic, minced
12-oz. tube refrigerated biscuits
2 T. grated Parmesan cheese

Coat the bottom of a 9" pie plate with butter; sprinkle with celery seed and garlic. Cut each biscuit into quarters; arrange on top of butter mixture. Sprinkle with Parmesan cheese. Bake at 425 degrees for 12 to 15 minutes. Invert onto a serving plate to serve.

★ DOUBLE DUTY ★ Homemade fruit butter is a delightful way to use a bounty of ripe fruit. It's scrumptious on warm muffins. Try it on waffles or as an ice cream topping too...even give a ribbon-topped jar for a gift anyone would appreciate.

Sour Cream Mini Biscuits

Jenny Sisson, Broomfield, CO

Cranberry Buttermilk Scones

Enjoy these scones fresh from the oven with a dollop of butter or as an afternoon snack with tea...they're a favorite any time you eat them.

Makes 10.

2 c. all-purpose flour
1/3 c. sugar
1/4 t. salt
1-1/2 t. baking powder
1/2 t. baking soda
6 T. butter
2/3 c. sweetened dried cranberries
1/2 c. buttermilk
1 egg, beaten
1-1/2 t. vanilla extract

Stir together flour, sugar, salt, baking powder and baking soda; cut in butter with a pastry blender. Stir in cranberries. In a separate bowl, combine buttermilk, egg and vanilla; mix into flour mixture until just moistened. Drop dough by tablespoonfuls onto a greased baking sheet. Bake at 375 degrees for 15 minutes, or until golden.

Jenna Hord, Mount Vernon, OH

Baking Powder Biscuits

My grandma and her mother used to make these tender biscuits...perfect for a hearty breakfast or supper!

Makes 15 to 18.

2 c. all-purpose flour
1 T. baking powder
1 t. salt
1/4 c. shortening
3/4 c. milk

In a bowl, sift together flour, baking powder and salt. Cut in shortening with 2 knives or a fork until mixture is as coarse as cornmeal. Add milk; stir just enough to make a soft dough. Turn out dough onto a lightly floured surface; knead for about 30 seconds. Roll out dough 1/2-inch thick. Cut out biscuits with a floured 2-inch round cutter. Place biscuits one inch apart on ungreased baking sheets. Bake at 450 degrees for 12 to 15 minutes, until golden.

★ DOUBLE DUTY ★ Use the open end of a clean, empty soup can to cut biscuit dough into rounds...there's no need to purchase a special biscuit cutter.

Cranberry Buttermilk Scones

Casii Dodd, Frederick, MD

Cheddar-Chive Muffins

Warm, cheesy muffins with fresh chives make a fitting accompaniment to a steaming bowl of chili or soup.

Makes about one dozen.

1 c. all-purpose flour
1/2 c. yellow cornmeal
1 T. baking powder
1 T. sugar
1/2 t. salt
1 egg, beaten
3/4 c. milk
1/2 c. shredded sharp Cheddar cheese
1 T. fresh chives, chopped
1 T. butter, melted

Combine flour, cornmeal, baking powder, sugar and salt in a large bowl; mix well and make a well in center of mixture. In a separate bowl, stir together remaining ingredients. Add to flour mixture, stirring just until moistened. Spoon batter into greased muffin cups, filling 2/3 full. Bake at 400 degrees for 18 minutes, or until a toothpick inserted in center comes out clean. Immediately remove muffins from pans. Serve warm.

Jennifer Savino, Joliet, IL

Grandma's Irish Soda Bread

This recipe makes 2 loaves...one to keep and one to give away!

Makes 2 loaves.

3 c. all-purpose flour
2/3 c. sugar
1 t. baking powder
1 t. baking soda
1 t. salt
1-1/2 c. raisins
2 eggs, beaten
1-3/4 c. buttermilk
2 T. butter, melted and slightly cooled

Sift dry ingredients together in a large bowl; stir in raisins and set aside. In a separate bowl, combine eggs, buttermilk and melted butter, blending well. Add egg mixture to flour mixture; stir until well mixed. Pour batter into 2 greased 9"x5" loaf pans. Bake at 350 degrees for one hour. Turn loaves out of pans and let cool on a wire rack.

★ TIME-SAVING SHORTCUT ★ A great way to keep brown sugar from hardening is to drop a slice of fresh apple in the bag...it absorbs extra moisture.

Cheddar-Chive Muffins

Jodi Griggs, Richmond, KY

Cherries & Cream Muffins

These sweet muffins sparkle with sugar topping and taste oh-so delightful!

Makes one dozen.

1/2 c. butter, softened
1 c. sugar
2 eggs, beaten
1 t. almond extract
1/2 t. vanilla extract
2-1/2 c. frozen unsweetened tart
    cherries, thawed, drained and
    divided
2 c. all-purpose flour
2 t. baking powder
1/2 t. salt
1/2 c. milk, divided
Garnish: additional sugar

In a large bowl, beat butter and sugar until light and fluffy. Add eggs and extracts; blend well. Add half of the cherries to batter; set aside. Combine flour, baking powder and salt in a separate bowl. Add half of the flour mixture to butter mixture with a spatula, then half of the milk. Add remaining flour mixture and milk; mix well. Fold in remaining cherries. Fill greased muffin cups 2/3 full. Sprinkle generously with sugar. Bake at 375 degrees for 20 to 30 minutes, until golden.

Valarie Dennard, Palatka, FL

Sweet Potato Cornbread

Savor this cornbread like my family does...smothered in butter and honey!

Serves 6.

2 c. self-rising cornmeal mix
1/4 c. sugar
1 t. cinnamon
1-1/2 c. milk
1 c. cooked sweet potato, mashed
1/4 c. butter, melted
1 egg, beaten

Whisk together all ingredients just until dry ingredients are moistened. Spoon batter into a greased 8" cast-iron skillet or pan. Bake at 425 degrees for 30 minutes, or until a toothpick inserted in the center comes out clean. Cut into wedges to serve.

Cherries & Cream Muffins

Jennie Gist, Gooseberry Patch

Lemon Tea Bread

Make this bread a day ahead to allow time for the flavors to blend.

Makes one loaf.

1 c. sour cream
3/4 c. sugar
1/2 c. butter, softened
2 eggs, beaten
1 T. poppy seed
1 T. lemon zest
2 T. lemon juice
2 c. all-purpose flour
1 t. baking powder
1 t. baking soda

Combine sour cream, sugar and butter in a large bowl; mix until fluffy. Add eggs, poppy seed, lemon zest and lemon juice; mix well. Combine flour, baking powder and baking soda in a separate bowl; mix well. Add flour mixture to egg mixture and stir well. Spoon batter into a greased 9"x5" loaf pan. Bake at 325 degrees for one hour, or until a toothpick inserted near the center comes out clean. Cool before slicing.

Nikki Booth, Kinderhook, IL

Healthier Cornbread

Good topped with jam or jelly too!

Makes 9 to 12 servings.

3/4 c. whole-wheat flour
1/4 c. all-purpose flour
1 c. cornmeal
1 T. baking powder
1 egg, beaten
1-1/4 c. 2% milk
1/4 c. canola oil
Optional: 1 T. ground flax seed
Garnish: honey

Line an 8"x8" glass baking pan with aluminum foil; spray with non-stick vegetable spray and set aside. Combine all ingredients except garnish in a bowl; mix well. Pour batter into baking pan. Bake at 350 degrees for 20 to 30 minutes. Cut into squares; serve warm with honey.

Lemon Tea Bread

Francie Stutzman, Dalton, OH

Italian Bread

We love this bread with homemade vegetable soup or spaghetti...it disappears very quickly!

Makes 3 large loaves.

2-1/2 c. water
2 envs. active dry yeast
2 t. salt
1/4 c. sugar
1/4 c. olive oil
7 c. all-purpose flour
1/4 c. cornmeal
1 egg white
1 T. cold water

Heat 2-1/2 cups water until very warm, about 110 to 115 degrees. Dissolve yeast in very warm water in a large bowl. Add salt, sugar and oil; stir well. Stir in flour; mix well. Shape dough into a ball and place in a well-greased bowl, turning to coat top. Cover and let rise one hour, or until double in bulk; punch dough down. Divide dough into 3 equal parts and shape into loaves. Place loaves crosswise on a greased baking sheet that has been sprinkled with cornmeal. Cover and let rise 30 minutes. Cut 4 diagonal slices in the top of each loaf. Bake at 400 degrees for 25 to 30 minutes, until golden. Combine egg white and cold water in a small bowl; whisk well and brush over loaves. Bake 5 more minutes.

Kim Hinshaw, Cedar Park TX

Beer Bread

When I was growing up, my grandma made yummy homemade bread. This version is quick & easy!

Makes one loaf.

3 c. self-rising flour
12-oz. can regular or non-alcoholic beer, room temperature
1/4 c. sugar
1/2 c. butter, melted

Combine flour, beer and sugar in a large bowl. Stir just until moistened. Pour into a greased and floured 9"x5" loaf pan. Drizzle with melted butter. Bake at 375 degrees for 45 to 55 minutes. Serve warm.

Italian Bread

Amanda Kisting, Dubuque, IA

Garlic-Cheddar Beer Biscuits

My family loves the arrival of fall, when these cake-like biscuits reappear on our table. They're perfect with any cold-weather dish...the aroma of the garlic warms the whole house as they bake.

Makes one dozen.

1/4 c. butter, sliced
6 cloves garlic, minced
2-1/2 c. self-rising flour
2 T. sugar
12-oz. bottle regular or non-alcoholic
    beer, room temperature
3/4 c. shredded sharp Cheddar cheese
1/4 t. Italian seasoning

Combine butter and garlic in a microwave-safe dish. Microwave until butter is melted, 30 seconds to one minute. In a large bowl, combine remaining ingredients and garlic mixture. Stir until moistened. Spray a 12-cup muffin tin with non-stick vegetable spray. Divide batter evenly among muffin cups. Bake at 400 degrees for 15 minutes, or until tops just begin to turn golden. Immediately turn biscuits out onto a plate and serve.

Jennifer Niemi, Nova Scotia, Canada

Apricot Quick Bread

Quick breads are one of the easiest ways I know to satisfy a sweet tooth! For bake sales, I usually double this recipe and make three smaller loaves. At our latest bake sale for a local animal shelter, we raised over a thousand dollars!

Makes one loaf.

2 c. all-purpose flour
1 c. sugar
2 t. baking powder
1/2 t. baking soda
1/2 t. salt
1/2 t. cinnamon
1 c. dried apricots, chopped
zest of 1 orange
1 egg
1/2 c. milk
1/2 c. orange juice
1 t. almond extract

In a large bowl, stir together flour, sugar, baking powder, baking soda and salt. Mix in cinnamon, apricots and orange zest; set aside. In a smaller bowl, whisk together remaining ingredients. Add egg mixture to flour mixture, stirring just until moistened. Spoon batter into a greased and floured 9"x4" loaf pan. Bake at 350 degrees for 55 minutes, or until a toothpick tests clean. For the most flavorful, moist bread, cool completely, wrap tightly and refrigerate for a day before serving.

Garlic-Cheddar Beer Biscuits

Stephanie White, Idabel, OK

Caramel Apple Muffins

An extra-special breakfast treat.

Makes one dozen.

2 c. all-purpose flour
3/4 c. sugar
2 t. baking powder
1/2 t. salt
2-1/2 t. cinnamon
1 egg, beaten
1 c. milk
1/4 c. butter, melted
1-1/2 t. vanilla extract
1/2 c. apple, peeled, cored and finely chopped
12 caramels, unwrapped and diced

Combine flour, sugar, baking powder, salt and cinnamon in a large bowl; set aside. In a separate large bowl, mix together egg, milk, butter and vanilla; add flour mixture, stirring just until blended. Stir in apples and caramels. Divide batter evenly among 12 greased muffin cups. Bake at 350 degrees for 25 minutes, or until tops spring back when lightly pressed. Serve warm.

Bernadette Reed, Berlin Heights, OH

Stuffed Pumpernickel Bread

This is absolutely one of our family's favorites...the warm cheese filling is irresistible!

Serves 6 to 8.

1 loaf pumpernickel bread
1-1/2 c. shredded Swiss cheese
1 c. mayonnaise
1 t. garlic powder
1/2 t. dried parsley
1/2 t. dried basil
1/2 t. dried oregano
1/2 t. dried thyme

Slice bread into serving-size slices, but do not cut all the way through the bottom crust; set aside. Mix remaining ingredients together; spoon mixture between slices of bread. Wrap loaf in aluminum foil; sprinkle with a few drops of water and seal tightly. Bake at 350 degrees for 30 minutes, or until cheese is melted.

Caramel Apple Muffins

Gladys Kielar, Whitehouse, OH

Garden-Fresh Garlic Chive Bread

A loaf of hot, buttery garlic bread makes any dish a meal.

Makes 10 to 12 servings.

1/2 c. butter, softened
1/4 c. grated Parmesan cheese
2 T. fresh chives, chopped
1 clove garlic, minced
1 loaf French bread, sliced 1-inch
   thick

In a small bowl, blend butter, Parmesan cheese, chives and garlic. Spread on one side of each bread slice.

Reassemble loaf; wrap in a large piece of heavy-duty aluminum foil. Seal edges, forming a packet; place on a baking sheet. Bake at 350 degrees for 20 to 25 minutes, until heated through.

Mary Gage, Wakewood, CA

Fluffy Whole-Wheat Biscuits

These homemade biscuits are scrumptious with a bowl of hot soup or any country-style meal.

Makes one dozen.

1 c. all-purpose flour
1 c. whole-wheat flour
4 t. baking powder
1 T. sugar
3/4 t. salt
1/4 c. butter
1 c. milk

Combine flours, baking powder, sugar and salt; mix well. Cut in butter until mixture resembles coarse crumbs. Stir in milk just until moistened. Turn dough out onto a lightly floured surface; knead gently 8 to 10 times. Roll out to 3/4-inch thickness. Cut with a 2-1/2" round biscuit cutter, or cut into squares with a knife. Place biscuits on an ungreased baking sheet. Bake at 450 degrees for 10 to 12 minutes, until lightly golden. Serve warm.

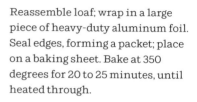

Fluffy Whole-Wheat Biscuits

Lori Vincent, Alpine, UT

Mother's Pull-Apart Cheese Bread

My mother always made this cheese bread for family get-togethers. Although she is no longer with us, I reach for this buttery, savory bread whenever I need to feel closer to her.

Makes 10 to 12 servings.

1 unsliced loaf white bakery bread
8-oz. pkg. shredded pasteurized
   process cheese spread
1/2 c. butter, softened and divided
1-1/2 t. onion, finely chopped
1 t. Worcestershire sauce
1/4 t. celery seed

Trim crust off top and sides of loaf with a long serrated knife. Cut loaf into 1-1/2 inch slices without cutting through bottom crust. Cut across slices from end to end, forming 1-1/2 inch squares. Combine cheese, 1/4 cup butter, onion, sauce and celery seed; spread between squares. Melt remaining butter; brush over top and sides of loaf. Place on an ungreased baking sheet. Bake at 350 degrees for 20 to 25 minutes, until hot and golden.

Connie McGuire, Madras, OR

Onion French Bread

A delicious accompaniment to soups and stews.

Serves 6 to 8.

1 loaf French bread, sliced in half
   lengthwise
1 c. mayonnaise
1/2 c. onion, chopped
1/2 c. grated Parmesan cheese
Garnish: paprika

Place bread on an ungreased baking sheet and set aside. Mix mayonnaise, onion and cheese; spread over cut side of bread. Sprinkle with paprika; broil for 3 to 5 minutes, or until golden. Slice and serve warm.

★ DOUBLE DUTY ★ The aroma of bread baking is so comforting, even refrigerated rolls will make your kitchen smell like baking bread. Dress up rolls with a drizzle of melted butter and a dash of dried oregano before baking...almost as good as homemade.

Mother's Pull-Apart Cheese Bread

Carrie Kelderman, Pella, IA

Pumpkin-Chocolate Chip Muffins

Most of us cook with pumpkin only in autumn, but these muffins are a welcome treat any time of year. Our family loves them!

Makes one dozen.

1 c. canned pumpkin
1/2 c. brown sugar, packed
1/4 c. butter, melted and slightly cooled
2 eggs, beaten
2 c. all-purpose flour
2 t. baking powder
1/2 t. salt
1 c. semi-sweet chocolate chips

In a large bowl, mix all ingredients in the order given. Spoon batter into paper-lined muffin cups, filling about 3/4 full. Bake at 375 degrees for 20 minutes, or until muffins test done with a toothpick.

Mel Chencharick, Julian, PA

Quick & Easy Walnut Bread

Add a handful of chopped dried fruit just for fun!

Makes one loaf.

1/2 c. sugar
1 egg, beaten
1-1/4 c. milk
1-1/4 c. chopped walnuts
3 c. biscuit baking mix

In a large bowl, mix sugar, egg and milk; fold in walnuts. Stir in biscuit mix; beat very well for about 30 seconds to a minute. Pour batter into a well-greased 9"x5" loaf pan. Bake at 350 degrees for 45 minutes.

★ DOUBLE DUTY ★ **Self-rising flour is handy for quick biscuits. If you're out of it, though, here's an easy substitution. For each cup needed, add 1-1/2 teaspoons baking powder and 1/2 teaspoon salt to a measuring cup, then fill the cup level with all-purpose flour. Mix well before using.**

Pumpkin-Chocolate Chip Muffins

Sharon Wood, West Columbia, SC

Sharon's Banana Muffins

I have used this recipe since my daughter was a baby...she enjoyed making these herself when I was teaching her to cook. She is now 29 years old and her children are learning to bake under my supervision too. Enjoy making your own memories!

Makes 8 to 10 muffins or one loaf.

1/2 c. butter, softened
1 c. sugar
2 eggs, beaten
3/4 c. ripe banana, mashed
1-1/4 c. all-purpose flour
3/4 t. baking soda
1/2 t. salt

Blend butter and sugar; add eggs and beat well. Stir in banana; set aside. Sift together flour, baking soda and salt;

add to butter mixture and mix until moistened. Fill paper-lined muffin cups 2/3 full. Bake at 350 degrees for 25 to 30 minutes. If preferred, use a greased and floured 9"x5" baking pan; bake for an additional 5 to 10 minutes.

Sandy Nobles, Petal, MS

Corn & Green Chile Muffins

Let a bandanna-lined basket of these spicy muffins star at your next chili supper...stand back and wait for the compliments!

Makes one dozen.

1-1/4 c. cornmeal
1/2 t. salt
2 t. baking powder
1 c. shredded sharp Cheddar cheese
8-oz. can creamed corn
4-oz. can chopped green chiles, drained
8-oz. container sour cream
2 eggs, beaten
1/4 c. canola oil

Combine cornmeal, salt and baking powder; mix well. Stir in cheese, corn, chiles and sour cream. Add eggs and oil; stir just until combined. Spoon batter into a muffin tin that has been sprayed with non-stick vegetable spray, filling each cup about 1/2 full. Bake at 400 degrees for about 20 minutes, until golden.

Sharon's Banana Muffins

Mary Gage, Wakewood, CA

Cornmeal-Cheddar Biscuits

If you really like the flavor of Cheddar, try making these biscuits with extra-sharp Cheddar cheese.

Makes one dozen.

1-1/2 c. all-purpose flour
1/2 c. yellow cornmeal
2 t. sugar
1 T. baking powder
1/4 to 1/2 t. salt
1/2 c. butter, softened
1/2 c. shredded Cheddar cheese
1 c. milk

In a bowl, combine flour, cornmeal, sugar, baking powder and salt; cut in butter until mixture resembles coarse crumbs. Stir in cheese and milk just until moistened. Drop dough by 1/4 cupfuls onto an ungreased baking sheet. Bake at 450 degrees for 12 to 15 minutes, until lightly golden.

Molly Cool, Columbus, OH

Country Potato Biscuits

A basket of warm biscuits turns any soup supper into a feast!

Makes one dozen.

2-1/4 c. biscuit baking mix
1/3 c. instant mashed potato flakes
2/3 c. milk
2 T. sour cream

Combine biscuit mix and potato flakes in a bowl; set aside. In a separate bowl, whisk milk and sour cream together. Stir milk mixture into dry ingredients just until moistened. Drop by heaping tablespoonfuls onto a greased baking sheet. Bake at 400 degrees for 10 to 12 minutes, or until tops are lightly golden. Serve warm.

Cornmeal-Cheddar Biscuits

Marlene Darnell, Newport Beach, CA

Pretzel Twists

Try shaping the pretzels into letters or numbers for a fun twist!

Makes 2 dozen.

2 16-oz. loaves frozen bread dough, thawed
1 egg white, beaten
1 t. water
coarse salt to taste

Divide dough into twenty-four, 1-1/2 inch balls. Roll each ball into a rope 14 inches long. Shape as desired; arrange one inch apart on lightly greased baking sheets. Let rise in a warm place for 20 minutes. Whisk together egg white and water; brush over pretzels. Sprinkle with salt. Place a shallow pan with one inch of boiling water on bottom rack of oven. Bake pretzels on rack above water at 350 degrees for 20 minutes, or until golden.

Cheryl Hagy, Quarryville, PA

No-Knead Jiffy Rolls

This is a beer bread recipe turned into rolls...these are delicious and simple to make.

Makes one dozen.

3 c. self-rising flour
3 T. sugar
1/4 t. salt
12-oz. can regular or non-alcoholic beer, room temperature

Mix flour, sugar and salt together; add beer and stir well. Spray a muffin tin with non-stick vegetable spray; fill cups 2/3 full. Bake at 375 degrees for 30 minutes, or until golden. Serve warm.

Pretzel Twists

Deb Young, Milford, IN

Pull-Apart Bacon Bread

A hearty burst of flavors...so good!

Serves 8.

1 t. oil
3/4 c. green pepper, chopped
3/4 c. onion, chopped
3 7-1/2 oz. tubes refrigerated
    buttermilk biscuits
1 lb. bacon, crisply cooked and
    crumbled
1/4 c. margarine, melted
1 c. shredded Cheddar cheese

Heat oil in a large skillet; sauté green pepper and onion until tender. Remove from heat; set aside. Slice biscuits into quarters; place in a bowl. Add pepper mixture, bacon, margarine and cheese; toss until mixed. Transfer mixture to a greased 10" tube pan; bake at 350 degrees for 30 minutes. Invert onto a serving platter to serve.

Michelle Mahler, Osceola, WI

Champion Banana Bread

My grandma taught me most of what I know about baking. This simple recipe was hers...I wish I knew where she got it! I even won the Champion Ribbon at the county fair with this recipe when I was a young girl. My family belongs to a little old country church and it has been published in their cookbook several times as well.

Makes one loaf.

2 eggs, beaten
1/2 c. butter, softened
1 c. sugar
3 bananas, mashed
1/2 c. evaporated milk
1 t. vanilla extract
1 t. baking powder
1 t. baking soda
1/2 t. salt
2 c. all-purpose flour

Blend eggs, butter and sugar; add bananas, milk and vanilla. Stir in dry ingredients; mix well. Pour batter into a 9"x5" loaf pan that has been sprayed with non-stick vegetable spray. Bake at 350 degrees for 40 to 50 minutes.

Pull-Apart Bacon Bread

Pearl Weaver, East Prairie, MO

Nutty Brown Sugar Muffins

With a flavor that's so much like pecan pie, these muffins are sure to become a new favorite.

Makes 10.

2 eggs, beaten
1/2 c. butter, melted and cooled
  slightly
1 c. brown sugar, packed
1/2 c. all-purpose flour
1 c. chopped pecans

Stir together eggs and butter. Add remaining ingredients; stir just until blended. Spray foil muffin cup liners with non-stick vegetable spray. Place liners in a muffin tin; fill 2/3 full. Bake at 350 degrees for 25 minutes. Remove muffins from pan immediately; cool.

Angie Venable, Ostrander, OH

Cheese-Stuffed Biscuits

My kind of recipe...down-home goodness, ready to serve in a jiffy!

Makes 10.

10-oz. tube refrigerated flaky biscuits
8-oz. pkg. Cheddar cheese, sliced into
  10 cubes
1 T. milk
1 t. poppy seed

Separate dough into 10 biscuits. Open a small pocket in the side of each biscuit; tuck a cheese cube into each pocket. Press dough together to seal well. Place biscuits on an ungreased baking sheet. Cut a deep "X" in the top of each biscuit. Brush with milk and sprinkle with poppy seed. Bake at 400 degrees for 10 to 12 minutes, until golden. Serve warm.

Nutty Brown Sugar Muffins

Berry Crumble, Page 232

CHAPTER SIX

Decadent Desserts

Friendship Peppermint Mud Pie, Page 236   **Soft Peanut Butter Cookies, Page 226**

Linda Jancik, Lakewood, OH

Creamsicles

Fresh orange juice makes these creamy frozen treats taste so much better than store-bought.

Makes one dozen.

1 pt. vanilla ice cream or ice milk, softened
6-oz. can frozen orange juice concentrate, thawed
1/4 c. honey
1-1/2 c. fat-free milk
12 treat sticks

Combine ice cream or ice milk, orange juice concentrate and honey in a large bowl; mix well. Gradually beat in milk; spoon into 12 small wax paper cups or an ice cube tray.Freeze; insert sticks into paper cups or ice cube tray when partially frozen.

Sherry Cecil, South Point, OH

Speedy Little Devils

When I was a child, this was my "special treat" that Mom made for me. Little did I know back then how just a few simple ingredients could make such a delicious rich dessert. Now that I have my own family, this has become one of my kids' favorite desserts and always takes me back to fond memories from my childhood!

Makes one dozen.

18-1/4 oz. pkg. devil's food cake mix
1/2 c. butter, melted
1/2 c. creamy peanut butter
7-oz. jar marshmallow creme

In a large bowl, combine dry cake mix with melted butter; mix well. Reserve 1-1/2 cups of cake mixture for topping. Press remaining cake mixture into the bottom of an ungreased 13"x9" baking pan. In a separate bowl, blend peanut butter and marshmallow creme; gently spread over cake mixture. Sprinkle remaining cake mixture over top. Bake at 350 degrees for 20 minutes. Cool; cut into squares.

★ TIME-SAVING SHORTCUT ★ Spray the measuring cup with non-stick vegetable spray before measuring honey, marshmallow creme or peanut butter...the sticky stuff will slip right out!

Creamsicles

Carol Nebzydoski, Pleasant Mount, PA

Peanut Butter Pie

My kids have always loved this creamy, peanut buttery pie. My 21-year-old son even called from Texas while he was in the army and asked for the recipe so he could make it for a small gathering of friends before they left for Iraq.

Serves 8.

1/2 c. sugar
1/2 c. creamy or crunchy peanut
    butter
3-oz. pkg. cream cheese, softened
12-oz. container frozen whipped
    topping, thawed
9-inch graham cracker crust
Optional: additional whipped cream,
    chopped peanuts

Combine sugar, peanut butter and cream cheese in a large bowl; stir until well blended. Fold in whipped topping. Spoon mixture into pie crust. Cover and chill at least 2 hours before serving. Top with additional whipped cream and chopped peanuts, if desired.

Judy Borecky, Escondido, CA

Judy's Brownie Cookies

My husband loves these cookies...and who wouldn't, with chocolate chips, cranberries and crunchy oats?

Makes 2 dozen.

20-oz. pkg. brownie mix
1-1/2 c. quick-cooking oats, uncooked
1/2 c. oil
2 eggs, beaten
1/2 c. semi-sweet chocolate chips
1/2 c. sweetened dried cranberries
Optional: pecan halves

In a large bowl, combine dry brownie mix, oats, oil and eggs; mix well. Stir in chocolate chips and cranberries. Drop dough by rounded teaspoons onto ungreased baking sheets. If desired, press 3 to 4 pecan halves onto the top of each cookie. Bake, one sheet at a time, at 350 degrees for 15 to 17 minutes. Let cookies cool for 2 minutes; remove to wire racks and cool completely.

★ TIME-SAVING SHORTCUT ★ Line baking sheets and pans with parchment paper cut to fit...cakes and cookies won't stick and clean-up is oh-so easy.

Peanut Butter Pie

Jenny Young, Galena, OH

Mocha Mousse Pie

This pie is so easy to make. I often switch up the flavors trying different flavors of pudding and coffee.

Serves 8.

1/4 c. mocha coffee drink mix
2 c. milk, divided
2 3.4-oz. pkgs. instant vanilla
   pudding mix
8-oz. container frozen whipped
   topping, thawed
9-inch graham cracker crust
Garnish: additional whipped topping,
   baking cocoa, chopped nuts

Blend together mocha coffee drink mix and 1/4 cup milk in a medium bowl; stir until well blended. Stir in pudding mix and remaining milk; whisk for 2 minutes. Fold in whipped topping; spread into pie crust. Refrigerate for one hour, or until firm. Garnish with dollops of whipped topping, a sprinkle of cocoa, or nuts, if desired. Store in refrigerator.

Melissa Fraser, Valencia, CA

Cinnamon-Sugar Crisp Strips

Once you taste these, you'll have trouble walking away from more! Try dipping them in warm cinnamon-apple pie filling.

Serves 6 to 8.

1 T. cinnamon
1 c. sugar
oil for deep frying
8 10-inch flour tortillas, cut into
   1-inch strips

Combine cinnamon and sugar in a bowl; set aside. Heat 2 inches of oil in a heavy skillet over medium-high heat. Add 5 to 7 tortilla strips at a time; cook for 20 to 40 seconds on each side, until crisp. Drain on a paper towel-lined plate for 5 minutes, then sprinkle with cinnamon-sugar. Place strips and remaining cinnamon-sugar into a paper bag. Gently toss tortilla strips to coat well. Remove from bag and arrange on a serving plate.

Cinnamon-Sugar Crisp Strips

Brenda Tranka, Amboy, IL

Soft Peanut Butter Cookies

If you're a peanut butter fan, these cookies won't last long. You'll enjoy every last crumb!

Makes 2 dozen.

1 c. sugar
1 c. creamy peanut butter
1 egg, slightly beaten
1 t. vanilla extract

Combine all ingredients; mix well. Roll dough into one-inch balls and place on ungreased baking sheets. Use a fork to press a crisscross pattern into the top of each cookie. Bake at 325 degrees for 10 minutes, or until golden. Let cool before removing from baking sheets.

Rebecca Etling, Blairsville, PA

Nut Macaroons

One of my favorite quick & easy cookie recipes.

Makes 2 dozen.

2/3 c. sweetened condensed milk
1 c. sweetened flaked coconut
1 c. chopped nuts
1 t. vanilla extract
3/4 t. almond extract

In a bowl, mix all ingredients in the order given. Drop by teaspoonfuls onto well-greased baking sheets. Bake at 350 degrees for 10 to 12 minutes, until dry around the edges.

★ FREEZE IT ★ **Whip up a cool fruit dessert...you won't believe how easy it is. Freeze an unopened can of your favorite fruit. At serving time, scoop out frozen fruit and process in a food processor until smooth.**

Soft Peanut Butter Cookies

Hope Davenport, Portland, TX

Pecan Bites

These sweet bites don't even need frosting.

Makes about 1-1/2 dozen.

1 c. brown sugar, packed
1/2 c. all-purpose flour
1 c. chopped pecans
2/3 c. butter, melted and slightly
   cooled
2 eggs, beaten

Combine sugar, flour and pecans; mix well and set aside. In a separate bowl, stir together butter and eggs; mix into flour mixture. Spoon batter into greased and floured mini muffin cups, filling 2/3 full. Bake at 350 degrees for 22 to 25 minutes. Cool on a wire rack.

Karen Ensign, Providence, UT

Rocky Mountain Cereal Bars

These homemade snack bars will disappear quickly!

Makes 2-1/2 dozen.

2/3 c. sugar
2/3 c. corn syrup
1 c. creamy peanut butter
6 c. doughnut-shaped multi-grain
   oat cereal
3/4 to 1 c. sweetened dried
   cranberries

Combine sugar, corn syrup and peanut butter in a large saucepan over low heat. Stirring mixture constantly, heat through until peanut butter is melted. Remove from heat. Add cereal and cranberries; mix well. Spread cereal mixture evenly into a lightly greased 13"x9" baking pan. Cool completely; cut into bars.

★ TIME-SAVING SHORTCUT ★
Bake a peach cobbler alongside tonight's dinner...it's so easy. Blend one cup sugar and 1/2 cup butter in a 9"x9" baking pan. Stir in one cup each of self-rising flour and milk and pour a 15-ounce can of peaches over top, juice and all. Bake at 350 degrees for 25 to 30 minutes, until golden. Mmm!

Rocky Mountain Cereal Bars

Shawna Brock, Eglin AFB, FL

White Chocolate-Cranberry Cookies

Dried cranberries taste surprisingly sweet. When paired with white chocolate, they'll make these cookies a favorite choice.

Makes about 2-1/2 dozen.

1/2 c. butter, softened
3/4 c. sugar
1/2 c. brown sugar, packed
1 egg, beaten
1 t. vanilla extract
1-3/4 c. all-purpose flour
1 t. baking powder
1/2 t. baking soda
1 c. sweetened dried cranberries
1/2 c. white chocolate chips

Beat butter in a large bowl with an electric mixer on medium speed until creamy. Gradually add sugars, beating until combined. Add egg and vanilla; beat until smooth. In a separate bowl, combine flour, baking powder and baking soda. Gradually add to sugar mixture, beating well. Stir in cranberries and chocolate chips. Shape dough into 1-1/2 inch balls; place 2 inches apart on ungreased baking sheets. Bake at 375 degrees for 14 minutes, or until golden. Remove to wire racks to cool.

Joyce Stackhouse, Cadiz, OH

Pumpkin Pudding

This recipe is really quick to make and scrumptious...perfect for a light dessert after a big meal. If you are watching your calories, you can use sugar-free pudding mix and skim milk.

Makes 6 to 8 servings.

2 c. milk
3.4-oz. pkg. instant vanilla pudding mix
1 c. canned pumpkin
1 t. vanilla extract
1 t. pumpkin pie spice
1/2 t. cinnamon
Optional: whipped cream

Combine milk and dry pudding mix in a large bowl. Beat with an electric mixer on low speed for one to 2 minutes, until smooth. Add pumpkin, vanilla and spices; mix well. Spoon into individual dessert bowls; cover and chill. If desired, garnish with dollops of whipped cream at serving time.

★ TIME-SAVING SHORTCUT ★ A real time-saver...double your sugar cookie recipe and freeze some of the dough in individual plastic bags. Thaw and bake for a quick, homemade treat.

White Chocolate-Cranberry Cookies

Sandy Bernards, Valencia, CA

Berry Crumble

Instant oatmeal is the key to the scrumptious topping.

Serves 6.

4 c. blackberries or blueberries
1 to 2 T. sugar
3 1-1/2 oz. pkgs. quick-cooking oats
　with maple and brown sugar
3 T. butter, softened

Toss berries and sugar together in an ungreased 9" pie plate; set aside. Add oats to a bowl; cut butter into oats until coarse crumbs form. Sprinkle crumb mixture over berries. Bake, uncovered, at 375 degrees for about 30 to 35 minutes, until topping is golden.

Darlene Hartzler, Marshallville, OH

Marbled Chocolate Bars

This super-easy recipe is a lunchbox favorite for my kids.

Makes 3 dozen.

18-1/4 oz. pkg. German chocolate cake
　mix
8-oz. pkg. cream cheese, softened
1/2 c. sugar
3/4 c. milk chocolate chips, divided

Prepare cake batter according to package directions. Spread in a greased 15"x10" jelly-roll pan; set aside. In a separate bowl, beat together cream cheese and sugar; stir in 1/4 cup chocolate chips. Drop mixture by tablespoonfuls over batter; cut through batter with a knife to swirl. Sprinkle with remaining chocolate chips. Bake at 350 degrees for 25 to 30 minutes, until a toothpick inserted in the center comes out clean. Cool in pan on a wire rack. Cut into bars.

★ TAKE IT TO GO ★ Yum...bite-size, chocolate-covered bananas! Just slice bananas and dip in melted chocolate. Freeze on a baking sheet, then store in plastic freezer bags, ready to pull out the next time you need a speedy treat.

Berry Crumble

Linda Kiffin, Tracy, CA

Ruby's Bavarian Cloud

Experiment with different gelatin flavors to make this recipe your own.

Serves 6.

3-oz. pkg. favorite flavor gelatin mix
1/4 c. sugar
1 c. boiling water
3/4 c. chilled fruit juice or cold water
1/2 c. milk
1/2 t. vanilla extract
16-oz. container frozen whipped topping, thawed
Optional: crushed graham crackers, chopped fruit, whipped topping

In a large bowl, combine dry gelatin mix, sugar and boiling water. Stir until gelatin is dissolved. Blend in chilled fruit juice or cold water, milk and vanilla; fold in whipped topping. Top with crushed crackers, chopped fruit and whipped topping, if desired. Cover and chill for 4 hours before serving.

Tina Goodpasture, Meadowview, VA

Tina's Marshmallow Pie

I love mallow cups and think of them whenever I serve this creamy pie!

Makes 8 servings.

10-oz. pkg. mini marshmallows
1/2 c. milk
1/4 c. butter, sliced
1 c. frozen whipped topping, thawed
9-inch graham cracker crust
Garnish: chopped chocolate pieces or chocolate syrup

In a saucepan over low heat, combine marshmallows, milk and butter. Cook and stir until marshmallows are melted. Let cool; stir in whipped topping. Spoon into pie crust. Cover and chill. Garnish with chocolate pieces or drizzle with chocolate syrup, as desired.

★ TIME-SAVING SHORTCUT ★ Top slices of bakery pound cake or angel food cake with fresh berries and dollops of whipped topping...what could be simpler?

Ruby's Bavarian Cloud

Lori Vincent, Alpine, UT

Friendship Peppermint Mud Pie

Minty chocolate ice cream cake with hot fudge topping...oh my!

Serves 12.

14-oz. pkg. chocolate sandwich
   cookies, crushed and divided
6 T. butter, melted
1/2 gal. peppermint ice cream
16-oz. jar hot fudge ice cream topping
8-oz. container frozen whipped
   topping, thawed

Set aside 1/4 cup cookie crumbs. Combine remaining cookie crumbs and melted butter in a large bowl; toss to coat. Transfer to a greased 13"x9" baking pan; press crumbs firmly to cover bottom of pan. Spread ice cream over crumb crust. Top with fudge topping. Cover and freeze until firm, 2 to 3 hours. At serving time, spread whipped topping to edges. Garnish with reserved cookie crumbs.

Brenda Austin, Durand, MI

Graham Cracker Deluxe

This creamy pudding dessert chills for several hours or overnight, so you'll want to allow enough time. Assemble it into individual parfait glasses, if you like.

Serves 12.

2 3.4-oz. pkgs. French vanilla instant
   pudding mix
2-3/4 c. milk
16-oz. container frozen whipped
   topping, thawed
1-1/2 pkgs. sleeves graham crackers,
   divided

Stir together dry pudding mixes and milk for 2 minutes, until mixture is thickened. Blend in whipped topping; set aside. Line a 13"x9" baking pan with a single layer of graham crackers. Spoon half of pudding mixture over crackers; smooth with the back of a spoon. Add another layer of crackers and remaining pudding mixture; smooth again. Crush any remaining crackers and sprinkle over top. Cover and refrigerate for several hours to overnight before serving.

★ DOUBLE DUTY ★ **It just wouldn't be dinner without dessert. Dress up bakery pound cake with a spoonful of cherry pie filling and a dollop of whipped topping...almost as good as homemade!**

Friendship Peppermint Mud Pie

Angela Sims, Willow Springs, IL

Peanut Butter Bars

With rich butterscotch frosting, these are no ordinary peanut butter bars...wow!

Makes 2 dozen.

1-1/2 c. graham cracker crumbs
1 c. butter, melted
16-oz. pkg. powdered sugar
1 c. creamy peanut butter
12-oz. pkg. butterscotch chips

Combine graham cracker crumbs, butter, powdered sugar and peanut butter; mix well. Press mixture into the bottom of a 13"x9" baking pan; set aside. Melt butterscotch chips in the top of a double boiler over low heat; spread over crumb mixture. Refrigerate; cut into bars when cooled.

Beth Richter, Canby, MN

Beth's Toffee Bars

This recipe gets taken everywhere! From the first time I made these bars, they have always been in high demand. At family gatherings, they often disappear as fast as they hit the table...they're that good!

Makes about 16 bars.

18-1/2 oz. pkg. yellow cake mix
1 egg, beaten
1/3 c. butter, melted and slightly
    cooled
6-oz. pkg. toffee bits
14-oz. can sweetened condensed milk

In a large bowl, stir together dry cake mix, egg and butter. Gently pat into a 13"x9" baking pan. Sprinkle with toffee bits; spread condensed milk over the top. Bake at 350 degrees for about 25 minutes. Cool; cut into squares.

★ TAKE IT TO GO ★ Do some family members need to dash off to soccer practice before dessert is served? They needn't miss out...spoon single servings of dessert into mini cups and refrigerate, to be enjoyed when they return home.

Peanut Butter Bars

Dottie McCraw, Oklahoma City, OK

White Chocolate Macaroons

Ready-made cookie dough makes these super simple.

Makes 2 dozen.

18-oz. tube refrigerated white
  chocolate chunk cookie dough,
  room temperature
2-1/4 c. sweetened flaked coconut
2 t. vanilla extract
1/2 t. coconut extract

Combine all ingredients in a large bowl; mix well. Drop dough by rounded teaspoonfuls onto ungreased baking sheets. Bake at 350 degrees for 10 to 12 minutes. Cool on baking sheets for 2 minutes; remove to a wire rack to cool completely.

Diana Diaz de Leon, San Antonio, TX

Slice-of-Comfort Pie

I hope you like this no-bake pie as much as I do! Halve the ingredients to make one pie.

Makes 2 pies; each serves 8.

16-oz. container frozen whipped
  topping, thawed
1 c. chopped pecans
14-oz. can sweetened condensed milk
16-oz. can crushed pineapple, drained
2 9-inch graham cracker pie crusts

Mix first 4 ingredients together; divide and pour equally into pie crusts. Place in the freezer overnight or until frozen.

★ SIMPLE INGREDIENT SWAP ★
For flavor and texture when baking cookies, butter is better! If you prefer to use margarine, though, be sure to use regular stick margarine rather than reduced-fat margarine, which has a higher water content.

White Chocolate Macaroons

Christina Mamula, Aliquippa, PA

S'more Dessert Please

Being on a budget doesn't mean you have to skip dessert!

Serves 6.

2 c. milk
3.9-oz. pkg. instant chocolate pudding
    mix
2 T. margarine
3 c. mini marshmallows

Stir together milk and dry pudding mix according to package directions. Set aside until thickened. Melt margarine in a saucepan over medium heat. Add marshmallows; stir constantly until melted. Pour mixture into pudding; mix well and pour into Graham Cracker Crust. Chill in refrigerator for at least one hour before slicing.

Graham Cracker Crust:
1 sleeve graham crackers, crushed
1/3 c. margarine, sliced

Place ingredients in a microwave-safe bowl. Microwave on high for 30 seconds, until margarine melts. Toss together well. Press into the bottom of an ungreased 8"x8" baking pan.

Anita Williams, Pikeville, KY

Fresh Fruit Kabobs & Poppy Seed Dip

Try grilling these kabobs for a new spin. Place skewers over medium-high heat for 3 to 5 minutes...yum!

Makes 8 to 10 servings.

6 c. fresh fruit like strawberries,
    kiwi, pineapple, honeydew and
    cantaloupe, peeled and cut into
    bite-size cubes or slices
8 to 10 wooden skewers

Arrange fruit pieces alternately on skewers. Serve dip alongside fruit kabobs.

Poppy Seed Dip:
1 c. vanilla yogurt
2 T. honey
4 t. lime juice
1 t. vanilla extract
1 t. poppy seed

Stir together ingredients in a small bowl. Keep chilled.

Fresh Fruit Kabobs & Poppy Seed Dip

Angela Lively, Baxter, TN

Super Fudgy Pie

Top with scoops of vanilla ice cream...yum!

Serves 6 to 8.

1/2 c. butter, melted and cooled
2 eggs, beaten
1 c. sugar
1/4 c. baking cocoa
1/4 c. all-purpose flour
1 t. vanilla extract
9-inch pie crust

Combine butter, eggs and sugar; mix well. Add cocoa, flour and vanilla; stir until blended. Pour into pie crust. Bake for 30 minutes at 350 degrees. Cool before cutting.

Ruby Hempy, Largo, FL

Tropical Treat Bars

Cut into oversize bars...cookie lovers will be grateful!

Makes 2 dozen.

1-1/2 c. graham cracker crumbs
1/2 c. butter, melted
14-oz. can sweetened condensed milk
1 c. sweetened dried pineapple, coarsely chopped
1 c. white chocolate chips
1-1/3 c. sweetened flaked coconut
1 c. macadamia nuts or almonds, coarsely chopped

Mix together graham cracker crumbs and melted butter. Press firmly into the bottom of an ungreased 13"x9" baking pan. Pour condensed milk evenly over crumb mixture. Sprinkle with pineapple, chocolate chips, coconut and nuts, pressing down firmly. Bake at 350 degrees for 25 to 30 minutes, until golden. Cool completely, chilling if desired. Cut into bars.

Tropical Treat Bars

Mary Patenaude, Griswold, CT

Easy Orange Cookies

Makes about 4 dozen.

18-1/4 oz. pkg. orange cake mix
2 c. frozen whipped topping, thawed
1 egg, beaten
Optional: 1/3 c. macadamia nuts,
    finely chopped
powdered sugar

Combine dry cake mix, whipped topping, egg and nuts, if desired. Form into one-inch balls and roll in powdered sugar. Place 2 inches apart on greased baking sheets. Bake at 350 degrees for 10 minutes, or until edges are golden. Cool one minute on baking sheets; remove to a wire rack to cool completely.

Edith Beck, Elk Grove, CA

Wild Blackberry Cobbler

A very old recipe that a friend shared with me in high school. Every year, we pick wild blackberries together so I can make this cobbler.

Serves 4 to 6.

1/2 c. butter, sliced
3 c. fresh blackberries
1/4 c. plus 2 T. water, divided
1-1/4 c. sugar, divided
1/2 t. cinnamon
2 T. cornstarch
1 c. all-purpose flour
1-1/2 t. baking powder
1/4 t. salt
1 c. milk

Add butter to a 9"x9" baking pan. Place in oven at 400 degrees until melted. Meanwhile, in a small saucepan, combine blackberries, 1/4 cup water, 1/4 cup sugar and cinnamon. Simmer over medium heat, stirring gently. Stir together cornstarch and remaining water until pourable; stir into berry mixture and cook until thickened. Remove from heat. In a bowl, mix flour, remaining sugar, baking powder, salt and milk; stir until smooth. Add flour mixture to butter in baking pan; carefully add berry mixture. Bake at 400 degrees for 25 to 30 minutes, until bubbly and crust is golden.

Wild Blackberry Cobbler

Miriam Ankerbrand, Greencastle, PA

Ice Cream Sandwich Cake

Why go to an ice cream parlor for an expensive ice cream party cake...you can easily make this yummy dessert at home!

Makes 12 servings.

12 ice cream sandwiches
8-oz. container frozen whipped
  topping, thawed
12-oz. jar chocolate ice cream
  topping
Garnish: candy sprinkles, crushed
  candy bars, crushed cookies

Arrange ice cream sandwiches to cover the bottom of a 13"x9" baking pan, using as many as needed and cutting some in half if necessary. Spread with whipped topping; drizzle with chocolate topping. Sprinkle desired garnishes over the top. Cover pan and freeze for about one hour, until whipped topping is firm. At serving time, cut into slices.

Debra Elliott, Birmingham, AL

Pineapple Pudding

This pineapple pudding is my favorite. It's an easy-to-make, mouthwatering dessert that will tickle your taste buds.

Serves 6.

12-oz. pkg. vanilla wafers, divided
1/3 c. sugar
3 T. cornstarch
1/4 t. salt
2-1/2 c. milk
1-1/2 t. vanilla extract
20-oz. can crushed pineapple,
  drained
8-oz. container frozen whipped
  topping, thawed
Garnish: pineapple slices,
  maraschino cherries

Layer wafers in a large glass trifle bowl until bottom is covered, reserving 8 to 10 for garnish. In a saucepan over medium heat, combine sugar, cornstarch and salt. Stir in milk. Cook, stirring occasionally, until mixture thickens. Add vanilla and cook for 2 to 3 minutes. Once mixture is thick, fold in crushed pineapple. Spread pudding mixture over wafers in bowl; let cool. Top pudding with whipped topping. Garnish with pineapple slices, reserved wafers and cherries.

Pineapple Pudding

Dusty Cannon, Paxton, IL

Tennessee Fudge Pie

Mama has always made this pie for our Thanksgiving. People request it for church socials and parties too...it's a chocolate lover's dream!

Makes 8 servings.

2 eggs
1/2 c. butter, melted and cooled
    slightly
1/4 c. baking cocoa
1/4 c. all-purpose flour
1 c. sugar
2 t. vanilla extract
1/3 c. semi-sweet chocolate chips
1/3 c. chopped pecans
9-inch pie crust, unbaked
Garnish: whipped cream, chocolate
    curls

In a bowl, beat eggs slightly; stir in melted butter. Add remaining ingredients except crust; mix well and pour into crust. Bake at 350 degrees for about 25 minutes, until firm. Cool before slicing; garnish as desired.

Carol Patterson, Deltona, FL

Blueberry Cream Pie

This delectable pie won me a blue ribbon at the county fair!

Serves 6 to 8.

8-oz. container sour cream
2 T. all-purpose flour
3/4 c. sugar
1 t. vanilla extract
1/4 t. salt
1 egg, beaten
2-1/2 c. fresh blueberries
9-inch pie crust, unbaked

In a bowl, combine all ingredients except blueberries and crust. Beat with an electric mixer on high speed until well mixed, about 2 minutes. Fold in blueberries; pour into unbaked pie crust. Bake at 400 degrees for 25 minutes; remove from oven. Sprinkle pie with topping; bake an additional 10 minutes. Chill before serving.

Topping:
3 T. all-purpose flour
1 T. sugar
1-1/2 t. butter
3 T. chopped pecans or walnuts

Stir ingredients together until crumbly.

Blueberry Cream Pie

Appetizers

Beverages

Biscuits & Muffins

Breads & Rolls

U. S. to Metric Recipe Equivalents

Volume Measurements

¼ teaspoon .... 1 mL
½ teaspoon .... 2 mL
1 teaspoon .... 5 mL
1 tablespoon = 3 teaspoons.......... 15 mL
2 tablespoons = 1 fluid ounce....... 30 mL
¼ cup................................. 60 mL
⅓ cup................................. 75 mL
½ cup = 4 fluid ounces.............. 125 mL
1 cup = 8 fluid ounces.............. 250 mL
2 cups = 1 pint = 16 fluid ounces .. 500 mL
4 cups = 1 quart.......................... 1 L

Weights

1 ounce................................. 30 g
4 ounces............................... 120 g
8 ounces............................... 225 g
16 ounces = 1 pound.................. 450 g

Baking Pan Sizes

Square

8x8x2 inches............. 2 L = 20x20x5 cm
9x9x2 inches.......... 2.5 L = 23x23x5 cm

Rectangular

13x9x2 inches.......... 3.5 L = 33x23x5 cm

Loaf

9x5x3 inches............. 2 L = 23x13x7 cm

Round

8x1-1/2 inches.............. 1.2 L = 20x4 cm
9x1-1/2 inches.............. 1.5 L = 23x4 cm

Recipe Abbreviations

t. = teaspoon   ltr. = liter
T. = tablespoon   oz. = ounce
c. = cup   lb. = pound
pt. = pint   doz. = dozen
qt. = quart   pkg. = package
gal. = gallon   env. = envelope

Oven Temperatures

300˚ F .... 150° C
325˚ F................................ 160° C
350˚ F................................ 180° C
375˚ F................................ 190° C
400˚ F .... 200° C
450˚ F................................ 230° C

Kitchen Measurements

A pinch = ⅛ tablespoon
1 fluid ounce = 2 tablespoons
3 teaspoons = 1 tablespoon
4 fluid ounces = ½ cup
2 tablespoons = ⅛ cup
8 fluid ounces = 1 cup
4 tablespoons = ¼ cup
16 fluid ounces = 1 pint
8 tablespoons = ½ cup
32 fluid ounces = 1 quart
16 tablespoons = 1 cup
16 ounces net weight = 1 pound
2 cups = 1 pint
4 cups = 1 quart
4 quarts = 1 gallon